shearer

Buddha

The Intelligent Heart

with 166 illustrations, 19 in color

Thames and Hudson

May all beings be happy!
May all beings transcend
The cause of their suffering
And be happy!

ART AND IMAGINATION

© 1992 Thames and Hudson Ltd, London

First published in the United States in 1992 by
Thames and Hudson Inc., 500 Fifth Avenue,
New York, New York 10110

Library of Congress Catalog Card Number 91-67309

Printed and bound in Singapore

Contents

Foreword

Go forth, O monks, to bless the many, to bring happiness to the many, out of compassion for the worlds; go forth for the welfare, the blessing, the happiness of all beings . . . Go forth and spread the teaching that is beautiful in the beginning, beautiful in the middle and beautiful in the end.

The Buddha

Twenty-five years or so ago, when I first became interested in Buddhism, there were relatively few books widely available on the subject, and they were for the most part introductory. Today, any good bookshop will offer a variety of Buddhist material: original texts, commentaries and interpretations from numerous schools, some popularized, others quite esoteric. Such is the profusion of words on the topic that paradoxically it seems time, once again, to present an overview of the teachings of the Buddha for those who may be interested in the subject, but have not yet developed any particular direction therein. I have had two aims in this book. The first is to present, in the text, the bare essentials of what is a vast and extraordinary body of transcendental knowledge. The second, in the illustrations, is to show how some of these teachings have expressed themselves through the cultures of a part of the world other than our own: in Asia, which contains the hidden shadow of the Western psyche. From studying this 'other', we may well meet the unknown within ourselves. One thing is certain: without this discovery, from whatever source, our life will be very incomplete.

'Turning the Wheel of the Law', the Buddha's first discourse, delivered in the Deer Park at Sarnath. Afghanistan, 5th century.

The Intelligent Heart

Imagine you have been shot with a poisoned arrow. You are lying on the ground, getting weaker and weaker, as your life-blood drains out of you and awareness ebbs away. You have a choice. You can either examine the arrow, asking yourself who fired it, and why, from which direction it came and of what it is made – this is the response of the philosopher or the theologian to the human predicament. Or you can pull the arrow out, immediately. This is the way of the Buddhist.

The human species is unique in its capacity for unhappiness; all of us, whether we realize it or not, have been shot with the poisoned arrow of suffering. So accustomed are we to its deadening effects that we have virtually ceased to notice them, accepting contraction and limitation as an inevitable part of life and seeking what satisfaction we can in the socially sanctioned activities of work, personal relationships, politics, or religion. But according to the Buddha, the world is on fire with suffering, both obvious and hidden, and the situation is urgent. Until we recognize this fact, and attend to the cause – the way in which the mind operates – we will never be able to establish just and happy societies, or realize our own birthright as peaceful, radiant beings living in harmony with ourselves and all around us. All our usual attempts to end suffering, whether personal or collective and however well-intentioned, are like the efforts of the prisoner who paints the bars of his cell gold: the bars may be gilded but the prison remains.

Though the problem of suffering is central to all the major religions, the Buddha is unique among the spiritual figures of history in that he never claimed to be a specially gifted or divinely inspired being, or a chosen prophet of God. In fact, he had no particular interest in becoming a world teacher, and always cautioned his hearers against accepting his words in blind faith. He merely asked them to measure his teaching against the yardstick of their own lives and their own experience and, if they found a correspondence, to continue inspecting and assessing their lives in the light of his doctrine. In this way, the seeker is led through a simple and direct process that presents liberation as the only intelligent or appropriate goal of human endeavour. On the few occasions the Buddha did speak about his own status, he usually likened himself to a doctor who examines the human predicament, diagnoses the illness and prescribes the cure:

> I show you on the one hand suffering, and on the other hand, the way out of suffering.

Whether or not we accept this analysis is entirely up to our own considered judgment. A phrase often used in the texts to describe the Buddha's approach is *ehi-passika*: 'Come and see for yourself.' If we do, what is involved is nothing less than a revolution in consciousness: the transcending of the limited individual sense of self. This radical shift in perception and the consequent state of being is the only cure for the suffering we experience and, wittingly or unwittingly, inevitably cause others. The core of true Buddhist practice, in no matter which of the many variegated schools that sprang up after the Buddha's death, is always rooted in the examination and understanding of our own mind. The *Dhammapada*, an early text dating from about two hundred years before Christ, opens with a statement of this basic point of departure in words whose simple clarity is the hallmark of the Buddhist perspective:

> What we are today comes from our thoughts of yesterday, and our present thoughts build our life of tomorrow; our life is the creation of our mind. If a man speaks or acts with an impure mind, suffering follows him as the wheel of the cart follows the beast that draws the cart.
>
> What we are today comes from our thoughts of yesterday, and our present thoughts build our life of tomorrow; our life is the creation of our mind. If a man speaks or acts with a pure mind, then joy follows him as his own shadow.

The question of causality is central to the Buddha's teaching. Popularly known as the doctrine of *karma* (a Sanskrit word meaning 'action'), the law of cause and effect means that the results of action inevitably return to the doer, sooner or later, due to the very nature of the dynamic forces operating throughout the universe. The idea of *karma* is one of the Buddhist concepts most familiar to the West, and indeed is found in Jesus' words: 'As ye sow, so shall ye reap.' According to Buddhism, whatever situation we are in at any one time is precisely the result of our previous actions, and therefore we are constantly provided with the opportunity to learn whatever lessons are necessary for our growth and development. Correctly understood, the doctrine of *karma* is thus not a way of avoiding responsible action, nor an excuse for a fatalistic acceptance of things as they are, but an incentive to deal with the present in the most positive and creative way possible; all experience becomes grist for the mill on our long journey to self-understanding.

Though the karmic configurations of any particular situation are nearly always too complex to analyse clearly, nothing exists that is not involved in its own cause. The inconceivable organization and beauty of the seamless web of life in which all phenomena are somehow mysteriously interrelated was something that fascinated many Buddhist thinkers. They developed the doctrine of the universe as an infinite 'Net of Jewels' in which each brilliant and many-faceted gem reflects all the others – an analogy of cosmic holism which would be acceptable to the findings of modern high-energy physics.

The chain of causality stretches through all time and space, and is the thread that links our various lifetimes together. All Buddhists believe in reincarnation, though on a day-to-day basis the subject probably occupies the average Buddhist as little as the topic of heaven occupies the average Christian. The doctrine of reincarnation is not merely an expression of wishful thinking, whereby the ills and mistakes of this life may be compensated by a happier and more successful time in the future. Some Tibetan schools specifically warn against the facile assumption that the next incarnation is bound to be a happy, or indeed even a human, one. In fact, it will be exactly as the effects of the actions of this life determine.

The rationale for what may appear to many Westerners to be an exotic or fanciful idea is provided by the Buddhist teachings on mind. According to them, all thoughts, feelings and perceptions are a form of energy, refined and subtle but energy nonetheless, and thus subject to the universal law that energy can never be destroyed but only changed into a different form. At the time of death, the grouping of mental formations that constitute what we call an individual mind leaves the disintegrating gross physical shell and moves to the subtler levels of creation. From here, at the time determined by its constituent elements, the bundle of mental tendencies will again return to the material plane as the seed-energy of whatever physical form is appropriate to the unfolding of its potential in the next incarnation.

Of all the Buddhist schools, it is the Tibetans who have most developed the teachings on the continuity of consciousness. Many high lamas are considered *tulkus*, conscious reincarnations of their predecessors, His Holiness the Dalai Lama being the best known of these in the West. One of the most extraordinary documents in the spiritual literature of the world is the *Bardo Thodol*, popularly known as the Tibetan Book of the Dead, which charts the course of the death and after-death process, and is traditionally read into the ear of the dying person to facilitate his or her transition to the after-death or *bardo* (literally 'intermediate') states.

Of the many recorded cases of remembered previous lifetimes that appear to stand the test of scrutiny, the majority have been found in oriental cultures where the belief is much more widely held than in the West. While the Buddhist idea of reincarnation does not involve a personal or individualized 'soul' that somehow partakes of eternity – the Buddha taught specifically against the idea of such a 'soul' entity – it nevertheless seems likely that some form of reincarnation was a widely held concept in much of the ancient world in the early centuries of the Christian era. In fact it was not until the Second Church Council of Constantinople, held in that city in AD 553, that belief in reincarnation was officially declared a heresy for the Christian.

The cycle of birth-death-birth is popularly known as *samsara*, a Sanskrit word meaning literally 'flowing together', often used as a synonym for the phenomenal realm of unenlightened and thus suffering experience. On an everyday psychological level, *samsara* also refers to the vicious circle of repeated patterns of thought, feeling and behaviour that keep us from growing and progressing beyond the boundaries of this realm.

No matter how the later teachings of Buddhism developed, the original message, as far as we can tell, is one of an emphasis unparalleled in the spiritual history of mankind. No parent deity to appease, no saviour figure to pray to, no gods demanding complicated rituals, no time-honoured customs to ensure divine protection. The responsibility for our lives is placed gently but firmly on our own mental and emotional tendencies and the behaviour patterns to which they give rise, and our salvation rests on our ability to purify and transcend them. It is in this unequivocal humanism that the Buddha stands unique in the traditions of the teachers of Universal Wisdom. The early texts are like deep pools of limpid water, cool and refreshing, but their ability to awaken us is only partly attributable to their chaste and elegant aphoristic style. The words of the Buddha touch us directly because they are our own true condition speaking to us through the medium of an apparent 'other', and this is the divine mystery and peculiar force of the spiritual master.

Miroku, the Buddha of the future age. Japan, 7th century.

The Life of the Buddha

The known facts of the Buddha's life are sparse. He was born about 560 B C as Siddhartha Gautama, the son of a king of the Shakya people on the border of India and Nepal. He lived and taught in one of the most spiritually fertile periods the world has seen, being roughly contemporary with the Greek philosophers Heraclitus and Pythagoras, the Persian sage Zoroaster, the Jain prophet Mahavira (who probably studied with the young Gautama) and, further east in China, Lao Tsu, who systematized the transcendental doctrines of Taoism in the classic *Tao Te Ching*.

Gautama enjoyed an undemanding life of consummate ease, grew up, married and had a son. So protective was his father, the story goes, that the young prince was forbidden to leave the palace grounds, in case he was faced with the ugly reality of everyday life. One fateful day, however, he did venture beyond the royal compound and on his journey he encountered four things that were to transform his life. The first was an old man, bent almost double, tottering along on his stick. The second was a man painfully ravaged by disease. Thirdly he saw, as one can still see in India today, a corpse, wrapped in simple white cotton, being carried shoulder-high through the bazaar on its final journey to the cremation ground. This encounter with old age, illness and death – known as the 'Three Marks of Impermanence' – shocked the naive young man to the core. Then, as he turned back to the palace, his eyes fell on a *sadhu* or wandering holy man, whose face radiated such a dignified and blissful peace that the young Gautama resolved there and then to renounce his existence of royal ease and devote the rest of his life to finding the Truth.

That night he stole out of the palace and began a spiritual quest which was to take him to study with all the most eminent teachers of his country. At first he followed the path of asceticism, practising austerities so ardently that, at one stage, so the texts say, 'he fasted so much that his navel touched his backbone'. Then, convinced that such practices were useless, he parted company with those who teach that the spirit can be reached by mortifying the flesh, and continued his search alone. After seven years, having studied the doctrines and heard the philosophies and practised the techniques of all who claimed to have reached realization, he remained unsatisfied.

Eventually his wanderings took him to Bodh Gaya, in modern Bihar, where, sitting himself under an ancient and venerable fig tree, he vowed not to leave until he had attained Enlightenment. During the next forty-nine days, seated in deep meditation, he repeatedly experienced and transcended all the levels of the mind, finally attaining full and complete Enlightenment, which is known in Buddhism as *nirvana*. Henceforth, he was known as the Buddha, an impersonal title meaning 'the one who is fully awake', or Shakyamuni, 'the sage of the Shakyas'. His teaching, born of disillusioned experience of the extremes of luxury on the one hand and asceticism on the other, is known as 'The Middle Way', or, more simply, the *dharma*, a Sanskrit word meaning 'the Law'.

From the time of his *nirvana*, which occurred when he was about thirty-five, until his death at eighty, the Buddha travelled extensively and energetically throughout north-east India, teaching and establishing monastic communities of both women and men. When he knew his death was near, he summoned the disciples who were then travelling with him, about five hundred in all, and, lying down under a tree, asked the assembled

The Buddha in meditation. Sind, 5th century.

The death of the Buddha. India, 10th century.

company if they had any last questions that they wished to put to him. There were none. The Buddha's final recorded words before he passed into what he called 'the great state beyond *nirvana*' (he was unwilling to define the status of the enlightened person after death) were to counsel his followers not to grieve for him, for:

> Decay is inherent in all compounded things. Live making yourselves your island, yourselves your refuge. Work towards your Enlightenment with diligence. (*Mahaparinibbana Sutta*)

The Buddha taught the *dharma* to all who came to him – men or women, high or low, king or outcaste. He taught in his own language, a vernacular dialect of north-east India, eschewing the priestly Sanskrit of the Hindu priests and pundits and, as his fame spread so far so quickly, he encouraged his disciples to learn his teachings in their own dialects. While he did not concern himself much with specific criticism of the existing political and social mores, it is worth mentioning that he did reject the institution of caste, then as now the glue of the Hindu social system, criticizing it as being susceptible to exploitation and conducive to prejudice. Nor did he condone the ignorant and fearful reverence he saw paid to the *brahmins* who, as the hereditary technicians of the sacred, enjoyed, and no doubt sometimes abused, their status as the pinnacle of the religious hierarchy. In his view:

> A man becomes not a *brahmin* by long hair or by family or by birth. The man in whom there is truth and holiness, he is in joy and he is a *brahmin*. (*Dhammapada*)

The Role of Authority

The Buddha was born into a civilization whose theological inventiveness is unequalled. But whenever he was questioned on such abstract subjects as the existence of the gods, or the nature of the afterlife, he tended to refer his listeners back to their own experience, warning them against unproductive metaphysical speculation or the acceptance of a doctrine merely because it was handed down by authority or sanctioned by custom. Similarly, while he never explicitly denied the existence of the myriad celestial energies that, then as now, are worshipped in India, he taught that uncritical acceptance of these, or indeed any other beliefs not based on direct experience, was inadvisable because it was not conducive to the end of suffering, which is Enlightenment. The picture that emerges from the early texts is of a supremely practical and compassionate teacher, whose concern is not to indulge the endless ways by which the mind evades the here and now, but rather to bring the student back to the simple consideration of the facts of his own restless life and the workings of his own dissatisfied mind. As he told Sariputta, a monk who allegedly attained Enlightenment after only two weeks in the monastic community (*sangha*):

> The recluse Gautama teaches the *dharma* on a system of his own devising, beaten out by reasoning and based on investigation. (*Majjhima Nikaya*)

That even his own words are not to be held up as some sort of unquestioned authority is made clear in a famous passage that recounts

Shakyamuni's visit to a town called Kesaputta. Here he is questioned by a group of families who are at a loss to decide which of the many teachings they have heard is in fact the true one. The pellucid assurance of the reply is typical of the tone found throughout the early texts:

> Yes, Kalamas, it is proper that you have doubt, that you have perplexity, for a doubt has arisen in a matter which is doubtful. Now, look you, Kalamas, do not be led by reports, or tradition, or hearsay. Be not led by the authority of religious texts, nor by mere logic or inference, nor by considering appearances, nor by the delight in speculative opinions, nor by seeming possibilities, nor by the idea: 'This is our teacher.' But, O Kalamas, when you know for yourselves that certain things are unwholesome and wrong and bad, then give them up . . . And when you know for yourselves that certain things are wholesome and good, then accept them and follow them. (*Anguttara Nikaya*)

The Essential Teaching

The problem of tracing 'the original Buddhism' has long exercised academics and scholars. Within a hundred years of the Buddha's death, no less than eighteen schools had appeared, each school adding its own emphasis or gloss on what it had inherited. Of these early schools, the Theravada or 'Doctrine of the Elders' spread to Sri Lanka around 250 BC and from there to much of South-East Asia. After the Islamic invasions finally drove Buddhism out of India in the eleventh century AD, Sri Lanka continued to be the main centre of orthodoxy and inspiration for the Buddhist countries of South and South-East Asia, and the Theravada scriptures, written in Pali, are by far the most numerous and complete of all the early collections. As their name implies, the Theravadins consider themselves the custodians of the true teaching. What the other early schools may have taught we cannot know for certain, as the only references to them are in the Theravada texts themselves, which are not objective in their criticism of their rivals. As time passed the doctrine grew and developed, and Buddhism today is a richly variegated tapestry of doctrines and practices that are congruent if not always superficially consistent.

Although generalizations cannot easily be made, at the core of all the various schools which have formed throughout the years lies an essential teaching that can legitimately be taken as the basic message of the Buddha. This was first enunciated in the discourse he delivered in the Deer Park at Sarnath, not far across the Ganges from Varanasi, a spot which even today retains an atmosphere of resonant tranquillity. It was delivered to his first disciples, five ascetics who had abandoned him in disgust years earlier when he forsook the path of mortification. The discourse is known as 'The Setting in Motion of the Wheel of the Law', and it revolves around the doctrine of 'The Four Noble Truths':

The Noble Truth of Suffering;
The Noble Truth of the Cause of Suffering;
The Noble Truth of the End of Suffering; and
The Noble Eightfold Path.

The Buddha teaching. Java, 8th century.

1 The Noble Truth of Suffering

Somehow, life is never quite as we would like it to be. Despite all our efforts, there seems to be something in the very nature of things that frustrates our desire to have everything 'just right'. This incorrigible perversity of life is an idea that is absolutely central to Buddhism. The Pali word for it is *dukkha*, a concept that has no easy equivalent in English. Usually translated as 'suffering', *dukkha* implies also 'impermanence', 'unsatisfactoriness' and 'imperfection'. The translation 'suffering' has created the popular misconception that the Buddhist outlook is essentially pessimistic, seeing life as a miserable and painful affair. In fact, in its analysis of the human predicament, Buddhism is calmly realistic, while in its vision of possibilities for human consciousness, it is gloriously optimistic. While there is undoubtedly a certain sobriety in the tone of the Theravada scriptures, this is not due to an inherent morbidity but to the fact that the Theravadins lived in monastic communities imbued with an unwavering desire for Enlightenment which rejects all evasion of uncomfortable truths or false consolation. The Buddha himself was by no means miserable; one epithet frequently applied to him was 'always-smiling', and the texts refer to his undisturbed tranquillity, born not of indifference but understanding. Representations of Shakyamuni in painting and sculpture invariably depict a serene and radiant countenance, devoid of any trace of gloom. Moreover, the consistent impression one gets from many of those cultures and individuals who practise the Buddhist way is one of a joyful and humane spirituality unburdened by doctrines of sin and guilt.

Of course, the Buddha never denied that there is much legitimate happiness in life, in work, family, friendships and so on, and the *Anguttara Nikaya*, one of the five Theravadin collections of his discourses, lists the different types of happiness available both to householders and to recluses. The point is rather that all experience, however happy it may make us at the time, is inherently unsatisfying because it does not last. Not only is the outside environment inherently unstable, but so is our 'body-mind' – our physical form, thoughts and feelings – which constantly changes.

Some of this constant change may be relatively obvious. We have all had the experience of the physical effects of ageing, or of the inconstancy of our political opinions or romantic affections. Change on other levels may not be so perceptible; the physical body that started reading this page is not the same as the one reading now. Your seemingly solid body is, in fact, a dance of energy in constant motion: ninety-eight per cent of all the atoms in your body are replaced in a single year, a new skin once a month, a new liver every six weeks, a new skeleton every three months, a new stomach-lining every five days, and so on. Added to which, this body, along with all the other energy in the universe, is recycled life after life, so that each of us now has in our body atoms that were once in the body of Gandhi, Hitler, Marie Antoinette and who knows who else. Nothing, absolutely nothing in the phenomenal universe is permanent. As the Buddha's contemporary Heraclitus declared, we cannot step in the same river twice.

The problem, from the human point of view, is that we crave the security of permanence. Without it we feel deprived of inner nourishment, 'dis-eased', and acutely aware of our own mortality. If we are enjoying something, we naturally feel upset when it comes to an end; in fact the very enjoyment of a situation can be compromised by the knowledge that it will

The Buddha as ruler of the world. Burma, 19th century.

not last. The desire for something permanent is in itself a natural enough thing – indeed it is this very impulse that can motivate us to seek liberation – but the problem is that we direct it to the outside world where, by definition, it can never be found. By clinging to the reality of our individual isolated 'self' we tend to identify with those things that appear to promise it security: the job, the social status, the bank account, the political party. Yet such externals can never provide ultimate fulfilment, being themselves inextricably part of the constantly changing kaleidoscope of life, and the bitter experience, or even the intuition, of this fact, is itself the cause of further suffering.

Nor does the remedy lie in retreating into some inner world of 'higher' or more 'spiritual' experience. The unsatisfactory nature of such consolation is made very clear in the passage in the *Majjhima Nikaya* – another of the early Theravadin collections – in which the Buddha includes even exalted spiritual states under the general classification of *dukkha*. Referring to those deep and gratifying levels of equanimity and mental absorption that lie far beyond what we would normally consider to be suffering, he says that, despite their benefits, such states are nevertheless 'impermanent, *dukkha* and subject to change . . .' because 'whatever is impermanent is *dukkha*'. It appears that whether we look outside or within ourselves, we fall prey to the error of misplaced ultimacy.

So there is this essential dissatisfaction, sometimes clear, sometimes hidden, but always there, like an itch we cannot scratch. And even if we are clever or fortunate enough to arrange our lives with an apparently satisfactory level of material comfort and emotional security, in the background there are always the 'Three Marks of Impermanence' with which the story of Buddhism began – old age, illness and death – and no amount of prudent living or skilful organization can banish these.

2 The Noble Truth of the Cause of Suffering

The Buddha located the cause of our predicament in what he called 'ignorance' (*avidya*) by which he meant a fundamental misperception about reality:

> I see no other single hindrance such as this hindrance of ignorance, obstructed by which mankind for a long, long time runs on, round and round in circles. (*Ittivutaka*)

Again the English term 'ignorance' is inadequate, as the concept of *avidya* is inextricably connected with the Buddhist insight that probably appears furthest from our own usual experience: the doctrine of 'no-self' (*anatta*). All of us live life egocentrically, and while we see our body as the outer limit of our self, we habitually refer to some intimate core of 'I' as the continuing inner self that persists through all our experience. This seems so obvious and so natural as to be beyond question. But what exactly *is* this ego, this separate sense of selfhood that motivates all of our actions and reactions? To the Buddha, it does not exist, but is in actuality an illusion, utterly dispensable. This little 'I' to which we are all so attached and which we spend so much time and effort cultivating, improving, indulging or disciplining, is only the minutest fraction of our real being, a superficial persona which, though necessary in our conventional social interaction, has no deeper reality. What we dignify as our 'self' is actually a moment-to-moment recoil from the infinite radiance that is our true nature and, equally, the universe at large, when perceived aright. This contraction into 'self', assumed by the infant and fostered by all the usual educational and socializing processes of human company, is a mortal (and thus fearful) crystallization of Unboundedness into a temporary and individual body-mind, and it is the identification with this contracted sense of being that is responsible for our chronic limitation and suffering. From the perspective of the individual ego, life is a problem to be resolved by an 'individual' standing over and apart from the 'outside world', a dilemma that seeks consolation through the repeated satisfaction of desire. Yet this whole alienated process, deeply rooted throughout personal and collective history though it is, is an illusion. For all its cool lucidity, the Buddha's message is an impassioned call to transcend this sense of isolated selfhood, to penetrate the nature of conditioned, ego-bound existence and discover the unlimited freedom that is *nirvana*.

To most of us, the proposition that we have no permanent 'I' is a manifest absurdity. Each day we wake up to reassume our sense of selfhood, and all our activity is impelled by it. How else could we live? Of course this centre is essential, our whole personality is organized around it and without it we would disintegrate into madness. The Buddha's answer to such common-sense objections would have been:

> Very well, what exactly is this self that is so dear to you? Is it your body, your thoughts, your feelings? Obviously not, because all of these, as we have seen, are subject to the universal law of impermanence. Is it then an individual soul, or 'Higher Self', as some religions and philosophies have claimed? If so, where can this 'Higher Self', or individual soul be located? Have you actually experienced it? Show it to me and I will accept that it exists.

The Buddha himself illustrates this point by means of the analogy of a house. What exactly *is* a house? You can point to the walls, the roof, the door, the windows and so on, but where exactly is the *house* itself? The answer is: it does not exist, save as a convenient verbal label to designate the totality of all the aforementioned components. Similarly with the self: our intrinsic sense of 'I' is in fact no more than a conventional and habitual label for the various factors that make up the personality. As a permanent entity, the ego with all its associated ideas of 'me', 'mine', 'belonging' and so on does not exist, and all the efforts put into consolidating, defending and preserving this 'self' only compound the error.

The Buddha's analysis was not intended as mere theory. Much of the practical discipline of Buddhism consists of meditation exercises designed progressively to undo the mental habits that keep us attached to the falsely imagined idea of 'self'. In Buddhism, it is axiomatic that a mind clarified by meditation sees things as they really are.

The Theravada texts painstakingly categorize the human personality into various ever-changing components which, in rapid and habitual combinations, come mistakenly to be regarded as an individual and indivisible 'self'.

These components are classified into five groups or 'factors', known by their Sanskrit name of *skandhas*:

1 *Matter*
This includes the external elements of solidity, fluidity, heat and motion; the sense organs, and their corresponding objects in the outside world.

2 *Sensations*
This group includes all the sensations, pleasant or unpleasant, that we receive through contact with the outside world through the sense organs. The category of sense organs includes the mind, which, in Buddhism, is treated as a sixth sense and which, like any other faculty, can be controlled and developed. Whereas the sense organs are concerned with gross objects – sounds, sights, etc. – the mind is concerned with subtle objects, such as ideas, thoughts and feelings.

3 *Perceptions*
These, like the sensations, fall into six categories corresponding to the sense organs and the mind. In the Buddha's terminology, a perception is the act of *recognizing* and *naming* any particular sensation.

4 *Mental formations*
In this group are classed all volitional acts, whether good or bad. By volition the Buddhists mean: 'mental construction, mental activity. Its function is to direct the mind in the sphere of good, bad, or neutral activities' (*Abhidharma Samuccaya*). This category is of especial importance because it binds the perceiver to the sphere of *karma*, and creates the attachment that propels the actor into further egocentric action and reaction. Among the fifty-two mental activities listed under the category of mental formations are such things as will, desire, energy, repugnance, and conceit.

5 *Consciousness*
This last category refers to the reaction or response that occurs to stimuli from one of the six organs (ear, eye, nose, tongue, body and mind) or one of the six corresponding external phenomena. Consciousness in Buddhism does not *recognize* a sensation (this is the job of perception as explained above) but registers it, and in so doing acts as the limited individual awareness. The Buddha explained this fine definition in some detail to a disciple named Sati, who had committed the error of confusing individual consciousness with an independent entity that transmigrates and experiences the results of good and bad deeds:

> Consciousness is named according to whatever condition through which it arises: on account of the eye and visible forms arises a consciousness, and it is called visual consciousness; on account of the ear and sounds arises a consciousness, and it is called auditory consciousness . . . .
> (*Mahatanhasamkhaya Sutta*)

Thus the Buddhist philosophical term 'visual consciousness' corresponds to what in everyday language we call usually 'seeing', and so on for the other senses and the mind.

It can be seen that in this analysis of the individual, there is no mention of a substratum of ego, soul or self. What we habitually and erroneously designate as a 'self' is only a conventional name or label superimposed on the interraction of the five *skandhas*. As Buddhaghosa, the fifth-century scholar and author of the *Visuddhimagga* ('The Path of Purity', a compendium of Buddhist doctrine) wrote:

> Mere suffering exists, but no sufferer is found; the deeds exist, but no doer of them is found.

It is this concept of a self operating behind the scenes, and its tenacious attachment to the ever-changing states conjured up by the play of the *skandhas* that is believed in Buddhism to be the root cause of our misunderstanding of the world and all our subsequent problems. The mechanics of how the self-concept operates is further explained by an analysis of causality. As we have seen in the general teaching on *karma*, everything that exists is the consequence of some other previous condition. This chain of causal connections, technically known as 'conditioned co-production' (*pratityasamutpada*), binds us to the contingent world of relative existence, life after life. Disentangling the knot of the 'self' and its operations was not merely a dry intellectual exercise. Alongside the rigorous investigation that the Buddha enjoined upon his followers went meditation practices that gradually and over time served to wean us from the limiting concept of being an isolated and individual self. In meditation the various levels and categories of *skandhas* are actually experienced and then transcended and it becomes clear that when the thought disappears, the thinking 'I' disappears along with it.

3 The Noble Truth of the End of Suffering

The Buddha. Thailand, 15th century.

The end of suffering is Enlightenment, *nirvana*. All of the Buddha's teaching is a means to our realizing this for ourselves, not as a philosophical theory but as a direct experience, a state of consciousness as different from the normal waking state as waking is from dreaming. It is precisely because it comes from a higher level of consciousness that his message may seem strange. It is as if a person who has reached the top of a mountain calls down to us below and describes the view; some of his description will be recognizable from our own perspective, but much will not.

Generally speaking, the Buddha was reluctant to describe *nirvana* in case his hearers adopted the description as yet another second-hand theory or belief. The most celebrated example of this reticence was the famous Flower Sermon, said to be the inspiration for the Japanese school of Zen. In response to a request to describe liberation, the Buddha merely held up a flower and remained silent. At best, words represent objects and concepts with which we are familiar, and we are not familiar with Absolute Truth; at worst, as the *Lankavatara Sutra* says, 'People get stuck in words as an elephant gets stuck in mud.'

In his style of presentation, the Buddha belongs to the *via negativa*, the way, found in all spiritual traditions, by which Reality is revealed by the negation of the unreal. In the context of the Indian tradition, such obverse reasoning (*apoha*) has a long and respected history. Thus many of the epithets describing *nirvana* are apparently negative terms, such as 'the ending of suffering', 'the extinction of craving', 'the Uncompounded' or 'the

Unconditioned'. This has led some critics to claim that *nirvana* is a state of negation, some sort of cosmic nothingness in which all true life is extinguished. Such misunderstandings are compounded by an ignorance of the syntax of Pali. Like Sanskrit, from which it is derived, Pali often expresses positive concepts by negations of their opposite, just as English does with such terms as 'immortal' or 'unstained'. The word *nirvana* literally means 'extinguished' or 'blown out', an allusion to the image of suffering egocentricity as a lamp fuelled by the oil of our unconscious and latent tendencies. As the *Digha Nikaya* puts it: 'The going out of the flame itself was the deliverance of the mind.' Whereas the world and the self are on fire with suffering, 'on heat' with desire, in contradistinction *nirvana* is often described by adjectives that carry the meaning of 'cooled'. Other common attributes of Enlightenment are: 'incomparable security', 'peace', 'freedom', 'the unchanging stability' and so on. As befits the Buddhist method, most of these definitions are formulated in psychological and human terms, not as metaphysical or ontological propositions. And while it cannot be described as an emotion, *nirvana* is nonetheless bliss, for, as the *Dhammapada* says: 'Nirvana is the highest happiness.'

In the context of the Indian tradition, the Buddha's approach was the opposite of the Upanishadic sages before him. They are fulsome in their descriptions of the Ultimate Reality, which they often refer to as the transpersonal 'Self'. Over the centuries, much has been made of this difference, particularly by partial defenders of the Buddhist position, but it is enough to see the disparity as one of approach and terminology rather than of fundamentals. Whereas the Upanishads positively celebrate the Absolute as the Unbounded Consciousness that pervades all, the Buddha's starting point was a careful dissection of the relative world, a dialectic which, taken to its logical conclusion, eventually reveals the Reality in which the world inheres. In his teaching on Enlightenment the Buddha is at one with the other great teachers of the Universal Wisdom. It is worth remembering that some of the most celebrated exponents of *Advaita Vedanta* (the culmination of the Upanishadic wisdom), such as Adi Shankara, were accused by their philosophical opponents of being 'crypto-Buddhists'.

The human personality is not obliterated in the transcendental realization, as some critics have feared. The *Anguttara Nikaya* lists no less than twenty-eight monks who are remarkable in some way for their individual characteristics; thus we learn that Sariputta loved solitude, Kassapa enjoyed austerities, and Vangisa was renowned for his wit. Nevertheless the enlightened being is another order of humanity, who sees and operates very differently from the normal social personality.

> Free from everything called form, he is deep, immeasurable, unfathom-able, just as a deep ocean.

One aspect of this freedom is that his actions are not motivated by egocentric concerns. As such they do not generate more personal *karma*, and therefore do not contribute to the necessity of further rebirths. Like all beings, however, the enlightened sage still receives the effects of the *karma* he has generated to date. Escape from *karma* is a contradiction in terms. *Karma* cannot be avoided, and anyway all *karma* contains the seeds of its own destruction.

The total sense of freedom that comes with letting go the concept of being an individual 'self' was pithily expressed by a contemporary master, the Thai monk Ajahn Chah, in a question-and-answer session with some of his followers:

> Consciousness is not an individual, not a being, not a self, not an other, so finish with that – finish with everything! There is nothing worth wanting! It's all just a load of trouble. When you see clearly like this then everything is finished.

4   The Noble Eightfold Path

The practical means for disentangling the knot of 'self' and its clinging habits is known as 'The Noble Eightfold Path'. This forms the heart of day-to-day Buddhist practice, and can be followed by anyone, monk or lay-person. The eight divisions, which fall into three sets, should not be considered sequential stages, but interrelated aspects of an integrated whole, each strengthening and reinforcing the others, like the spokes of a wheel united at the empty hub:

Right Understanding		Right Effort	
Right Thought	Wisdom	Right Mindfulness	Joy
		Right Meditation	
Right Speech			
Right Action	Morality		
Right Livelihood			

Right Understanding is concerned with learning to see the relevance of the Buddhist analysis to oneself and others, and gradually being able to see the world as it really is, moment to moment, without preconception, expectation or false imagining.

Right Thought becomes increasingly important as one begins to realize the power of thought on oneself and others, and the way in which whatever one focuses attention on, positive or negative, gains more life.

Right Speech concerns knowing what to say, how best to say it, and knowing when to remain silent. The Buddha was once questioned by a self-righteous vegetarian about the morality of eating meat. He replied that what comes out of our mouth is more important than what goes into it.

Right Action includes the guidelines on behaviour known as 'The Five Precepts':

1   Not intentionally taking the life of any living creature
2   Not taking anything which is not freely given
3   Not indulging in irresponsible sexual behaviour
4   Not speaking falsely, abusively or maliciously
5   Not consuming alcohol or drugs

In order to distance them from the *karma* involved in killing animals, members of the *sangha* were encouraged to be vegetarian, but as mendicants dependent on the lay community for their food, they were taught to accept whatever food they were given, meat or otherwise. Intoxicants were proscribed because they dull the faculty of discrimination and damage the subtle body.

The Buddha dispelling fear. India, 5th century.

The Five Precepts are recommended to everybody. Committing oneself to trying to observe them forms the major part of the simple ceremony performed when one becomes a lay Buddhist by 'Taking Refuge' with the 'Three Jewels of Buddhism': the Buddha, the *dharma* and the *sangha*.

The importance of right action is not only limited to the manifest realm. Each action implicates not only our immediate environment and those around us, but also all those beings touched by its unseen effects, which are incalculable. Moreover, as the effects of everything that we do, good or bad, eventually come back to us through the physics of the universal law of *karma*, it is only good sense to act in a way that is life-supporting and not harmful.

Right Livelihood is concerned with earning a living in a way that benefits not only oneself but the environment and all beings as well. We should work at something that is conducive to peace, understanding and happiness and not just something that amasses the most money, status or power.

These first five aspects of the Path are primarily concerned with the outward movement of consciousness, and can be seen to be very similar to the teachings on practical morality found in all the major religions. The remaining three are more to do with the subtle, inner movement of consciousness and the practice of meditation, through which the whole Path is nourished and invigorated. The general Buddhist term for what English calls 'meditation' is *bhavana*, a word rich in associations and best translated as 'culturing the mind'. As Buddhism developed, the various schools evolved very many techniques of meditation and visualization, but the last three stages of the Path contain all the essential practices in seed form. Mastering any one of them would establish an unshakeable footing in the cultivation of awareness.

Right Effort includes the determination needed to recognize and transcend one's habitual boundaries, resistances and negativity, and the perseverance needed to foster openness, understanding and positivity. It is self-discipline, not in the sense of straining to impose some rigid control, but in developing a patient and good-humoured recognition of the ways in which the mind clings to what it thinks will provide it with security, or evades facing a difficult truth. An important part of right effort is the ability to laugh at oneself; the Buddhist path may be serious but it is never solemn.

Right Mindfulness is essentially the practice of cultivating awareness of what one is doing, thinking and feeling at all times in daily life. The Buddha was once asked why his followers glowed with happiness, to which he replied:

> They do not repent the past, they do not brood over the future. They live in the present, and that is why they are radiant.

The most important single text on this subject is the 'Establishment of Mindfulness' (*Mahasatipatthana Sutta*), in which the Buddha delineates the four areas to which mindfulness (*sati*) should be directed: the operations of the body, our feelings and sensations, the movement of the mind and various topics of consideration. A common way to begin the practice of mindfulness is to focus attention on the breathing, so that one is aware of each breath as it comes in, momentarily rests and then goes out again. This may sound easy, but it is astonishing how quickly the mind shies away from

Kannon, bodhisattva of compassion. Japan, 8th century.

even such a simple act of observation, drifting off into fantasies, memories and all sorts of internal dialogue. In the application of mindfulness there should be no clinging, no judgments, no justifications, no regrets, no blame. Just simple observation and letting go. Everything that comes into awareness is seen as arising and, after some time, disappearing. In the practice of mindfulness there is no concern with what has been or what is yet to come, just uncluttered awareness of what *is* in the present moment, as direct, vital experience, freed from verbal labels and concepts. In the Buddha's words:

> A monk, when walking, knows that he is walking, when standing, knows that he is standing, when sitting, knows that he is sitting, when lying down, knows that he is lying down. In whatever way his body is disposed, he knows that that is how it is . . . . (*Mahasatipatthana Sutta*)

Such an awareness, unlike rational thought, is not attached to the outcome of any observation. Simple yet potentially awesome, it can give rise to the pristine state unstained by self. Continued observation will create a tranquil space in the mind, a quiet openness which can be brought to bear on whatever confronts us.

The development of *bhavana* is not mechanical or automatic in Buddhism. Awareness must be grounded with understanding for, as the *Samyutta Nikaya* says: 'He who has both meditation and understanding is close to *nirvana*.' Mindfulness is only the first requisite of a more comprehensive aspect of *bhavana* known as 'insight' (*vipassana*), in which a penetrating insight into the nature and structure of experience is nurtured by various practices. These help one 'look at one's mind as one looks at one's face in a mirror'. They include a causal analysis of the origin and effects of desire as it occurs from moment to moment, contemplation of the 'Three Marks of Impermanence', various deliberate manipulations of perception, and so on. Nor is 'understanding' a merely intellectual affair. According to Shakyamuni, for a person to become perfect two qualities should be equally developed: wisdom and compassion. The qualities of the heart are every bit as important as the qualities of the mind, and each goes to strengthen the other. A great deal of Buddhist endeavour is centred on the cultivation of loving-kindness (*metta*) and concern for the welfare of others, a concern that springs naturally from the teaching on *dukkha* and 'no-self'. Perhaps the easiest way to outgrow ourselves is through the response of compassion, that sensitivity which arises from the awareness of non-separation in the face of suffering.

Right Meditation, the last aspect of the Path, is concerned with the deepening states of tranquillity that open up as the mind becomes increasingly silent. Known technically in the Pali canon as: 'the four stages with form' (*rupa-jhanas*) and 'the four stages without form' (*arupa-jhanas*) they comprise successive levels of introverted attention: joy, equanimity, and mindfulness, giving way to different types of unboundedness culminating in the level of 'no-thing-ness' and the level of 'neither perception nor non-perception'. Thus meditation in Buddhism is not primarily the exercise of discursive thinking, though that may sometimes be employed as a starting point. It is more concerned with the gradual settling of mental activity until the mind dissolves into infinity.

The most complete description of the transcendental state born of meditation is found in the following words of the Buddha:

> There is, O monks, that plane where there is neither extension, nor . . . motion, nor the plane of infinite ether, nor that of neither perception nor non-perception, neither this world nor another, neither the moon nor the sun. Here, O monks, I say that there is no coming or going or remaining or deceasing or arising, for this plane itself is called *nirvana*, without support, without continuance, without mental objects – this is itself the end of suffering.
>
> There is, O monks, an unborn, not become, not made, uncompounded, and were it not, O monks, for this unborn, not become, not made, uncompounded, no escape could be shown here for what is born, has become, is made, is compounded. But because there is, monks, an unborn, not become, not made, uncompounded, therefore an escape can be shown for what is born, has become, is made, is compounded. (*Udana*)

It can be seen that the methods and goals of Buddhist meditation are very similar to what Christianity calls 'contemplation' or 'ascetic prayer'. The classical Buddhist descriptions of the various stages on the inner journey accord closely with descriptions in the writings of the great mystics of both East and West, such as St Theresa of Avila, Maharishi Patanjali, and Meister Eckhart.

It is worth remembering that the Buddha always cautioned his followers that any expanded state, no matter how exalted, was itself created by the mind and thus conditioned (*samkhata*). Attachment to any high state, no matter how pleasurable it may be, is still attachment, and as such stands in the way of Truth. This caution applies also to the supernormal powers (*siddhis*) that can come as the result of prolonged meditation. A typical story concerns the yogi who approached the Buddha as he walked by the river one day, proudly explaining that after twenty years of arduous practice he had eventually gained the ability to walk on water. 'Very good,' was the Buddha's response, 'but tell me, why have you spent twenty years cultivating this ability when there is a ferry just over there?'

A teacher holding scriptures. China, 14th century.

The Early Texts

At the first Buddhist Council, held immediately after Shakyamuni's death, no successor was appointed; only the *dharma* was left to guide the community. The entire corpus of teaching was said to have been recited by Ananda, the favourite disciple, and for four hundred years nothing was written down – in time-honoured Indian tradition, an oral teaching was considered less susceptible to misinterpretation and distortion. The cultivation of a prodigious memory has always been an indispensable part of Buddhist monastic discipline – just as it was in Vedic India or medieval Europe – and the records of the Buddha's words were chanted aloud, to become part of the very fibre of the monks' consciousness.

From the earliest time the material was divided into two main sections: the teaching (*dharma*) and the monastic rule (*vinaya*). These early collections display mnemonic traits typical of such traditions: a fondness for repetition, numerical lists and rhyming verse. Perhaps two hundred years after the death of the Buddha, a third category of text began to crystallize: the *Abhidharma* or 'superior *dharma*', that deals with more advanced doctrines and techniques for the cultivation of wisdom and insight. In their thorough but rather dry organization, much of these early works show the unmistakeable stamp of the monk Sariputta, who has been termed 'the St Paul of Buddhism'. Throughout the Buddhist corpus there is a further, somewhat hieratic division between two types of text. The *sutras* (Pali: *suttas*) are held to be the actual words of Shakyamuni himself, and will begin with the narrator Ananda saying: 'Thus have I heard. At one time the Lord dwelt at . . . .' Many alleged *sutras* were actually composed centuries after the Buddha died, and the authenticity of such works has remained a lively source of controversy among the various sects to this day. The other category is known as the *shastras*, which are systematic treatises written by later canonical experts who base their work on the authority of the *sutras*.

The Development of the Mahayana

At the Great Council of Pataliputra in 340 BC, one of the gatherings held regularly to reiterate the doctrine and assess the organization of the faith, the seeds were sown of a profound expansion in the teachings of Buddhism. A rift occurred between the Sthaviras, 'those who adhere to the teaching of the Elders', representing the orthodox monks, and the Mahasanghikas, 'those who represent the majority', a group of monks who supported the views of the lay community. The descendants of the Sthaviras were the Theravadins, whose importance to early Buddhism we have already seen. The Mahasanghikas, in their turn, gave rise to a number of schools that, by the beginning of the Christian era, were homogeneous enough to be known as the Mahayana. 'Mahayana' means 'the great ferry-boat', in contradistinction to the Theravada, which they disparagingly dubbed the Hinayana, or 'the little ferry-boat', the implication being that the Mahayana was able to carry far more people to the farthest shore of Enlightenment than the restrictive and reclusive Theravada. Throughout the subsequent history of Buddhism there has been a lively divergence between these two viewpoints. The Theravada considers that the Mahayana departed from the purity of the Buddha's original teaching, the Mahayana maintains that the orthodox failed to unfold the full potential of the *dharma*, an oversight which, as a Chinese Mahayana text graphically puts it, is like 'playing one's zither with the tuning pegs glued'. The wide variety in interpretations of the Buddha's message has led some to claim that he taught on different levels at different times, according to the capacity of his audience and the demands of the situation. Even allowing for this skilful use (*upaya*) of provisional truth, in general Buddhism demonstrates the law that the longer time elapses after the death of the teacher, the greater variety will be found in his teaching.

The Mahayana was to revolutionize Buddhism. Partly a reaction against the Theravada's tendency to indulge in dry scholasticism, its reclusive austerity and its disparaging dismissals of everyday reality, the Mahayana was also the joyous proclamation of a new and expanded vision of the universe, a revelation that has given the world its most breathtaking and audacious philosophy. Accepting all the basic Theravadin teachings on suffering, impermanence and 'no-self', the Mahayana sages took them a stage further. The original schools had revealed Enlightenment to be a subjective, individual freedom from all the limitations and restrictions of the external world of conditioned activity – *nirvana* is seen as the 'extinction of passion, of aversion, of craving, of confusion' (*Samyutta Nikaya*). The new wisdom schools taught that just as the subjective consciousness is realized to be unbounded and empty of self, so too is the whole universe. It is as if the inner freedom and unobstructed clarity of *nirvana* now begins to overflow through the mind and the senses into the outside world, illuminating and transforming everything we perceive. Not only is our own nature experienced as infinite, but the real nature of everything we see, perceive and feel is also infinite. All boundaries are now subsumed in an all-embracing unity, of which they are but the evanescent and non-binding modifications. Not only the individual, but the entire cosmos is seen to be the play of an infinite expanse, an unboundedness in which all conditions (including the individual body-mind) arise, in which they all adhere and are sustained while they pass through their changes, and into which they eventually disappear. Each object in the universe is now seen to possess the 'Buddha Nature', the timeless, spaceless dimension.

The Mahayana coined many terms for this all-pervading immensity: 'emptiness' (*shunyata*), 'the Void', 'Mind-only', and so on. To the miraculous perception of the enlightened, the world still exists but is transformed from something limited, heavy and solid to something fluid and extraordinarily spacious, a radiant dance of light, likened variously to a mirage in summer, the reflection of the moon in water, a dream, a fairy-tale city, a rainbow. In the unified vision, when all forms have become transparent to the formless, they become simultaneously negligible and infinitely precious. The sixteenth incarnation of the Gyalwa Karmapa, the leader of the Kargyudpa (Black Hat) school of Tibet, once described this unified state of awareness:

> All things in their nature are of the Mind. Being of the Mind, there is nothing, not even the tiniest thing like an atom or a mote of dust which is not of the same Mind nature. All is nakedly pure, unmade by Mind . . . uncompounded.

When it is described in its role of irradiating the world of particulars, the Void is known as 'suchness' (*tathata*), or 'things just as they really are' (*yathabhutam*). The affective reflex of seeing things as they really are is compassion. 'When thought is realized as Void and Compassion indistinguishable, that indeed is the teaching of the Buddha, of the *dharma*, of the assembly of monks' (*Advayavajrasamgraha*). The Theravadin ideal was the *arhat*, the individual monk who has achieved Enlightenment and enjoys a solitary and tranquil existence, but the Mahayana saw this as far too restricted a vision, and developed the ideal of the *bodhisattva* – 'pure-minded one' – a compassionate hero who, not content with his own salvation, resolves to do everything he can to lead countless beings to Enlightenment, no matter what the consequences may be for his own development. When asked what being a Buddhist meant to him, Tenzin Gyatso, the fourteenth and present Dalai Lama replied:

> For as long as space endures, and for as long as living beings remain, until then may I, too, abide to dispel the misery of the world.

In his dealings with those he comes across the *bodhisattva* is like a loving parent dealing with the fears of a child. Through his compassion he takes their problems seriously, even though he sees that, in reality, they are quite imaginary, being the result of a basic misapprehension about the true nature of both the self and the world. One Mahayana text compares the light shed by an *arhat* and by a *bodhisattva* to the difference between that shed by a glow-worm and by the sun.

The general tone of the Mahayana teaching is often more relaxed and celebratory, more suited to those trying to live in the world beyond the monastery walls. Thus sexual desire, for example, always a thorny problem for those with spiritual aspirations, is usually treated understandingly, as in the following Tibetan story. Two monks, one young and ardent and the other older and more experienced, were walking by a river. They met a beautiful young woman who had hurt her leg and didn't have the strength to wade to the other side. Much to the young monk's horror, his senior promptly picked the girl up and carried her across. The two continued along the other side, the younger one saying nothing, but barely able to stifle his indignation. Eventually, after about half an hour, he could contain himself no longer and burst out: 'How could you carry that woman across the river? You know it is strictly against our vow of celibacy to have anything to do with them.' To which his companion calmly replied, 'I put her down half an hour ago, but you are still carrying her.'

The generosity of spirit that characterizes the Mahayana is seen in its philosophical stance also. The Mahayana sages delighted in juggling verbal concepts in such a way as to make the logic of everyday, unenlightened perception stand on its head. Thus all the dualistic concepts recognized by the Theravadin analysis of suffering – transitoriness and permanence, conditioned and unconditioned, purity and impurity – are at some stage refuted in the light of pure knowledge. Even meditation, the essential plank of Theravadin equanimity, is redefined, as in this Chinese text:

> Know only that in the real nature of meditation there is neither stillness nor movement, and you will attain to the perfect meditation that gives rise to nothing at all. (*Vajrasamadhi Sutra*)

In the most irreverent schools, such as Tantra and Zen, even the fundamental and sacred opposition of *samsara* and *nirvana* is jettisoned. One of the most famous Tantric texts, originally from north-east India but best known in its Tibetan translation, is called 'The Treasury of Songs'. Attributed to Saraha, one of the eighty-four 'perfected ones' (*mahasiddhas*) whose teachings shaped Buddhism in Tibet, this lengthy verse poem celebrates the unspeakable paradox of ultimate attainment, in which one is freed from all identification and from all attachment, even to Truth itself:

> Here there is no beginning, no middle, no end,
> Neither *samsara* nor *nirvana*.
> In this state of highest bliss,
> There is neither self nor other . . .
> As is *nirvana* so is *samsara*,
> Do not think there is any distinction,

Manjushri, bodhisattva of discrimination, on an elephant. Japan, 18th century.

Yet it possesses no single nature,
For I know it as quite pure . . .
He who clings to the Void and neglects compassion
Does not reach the highest stage,
But he who practises only compassion
Gains not release from the toils of existence.
He, however, who is strong in the practice of both,
Remains neither in *samsara* nor *nirvana*!

The Mahayana's re-evaluation of such concepts as meditation, *nirvana* and *samsara* is easily misunderstood, particularly in times when there is general ignorance about the traditions of Higher Wisdom. Such a radical vision is born of utter dispassion, in which the everyday world of form is so shot through with the formless that the two are one, and in which all conventional models of 'ignorance' versus 'liberation' are seen to be an opposition of two mutually interdependent verbal labels that no longer have any independent reality. The existential 'problem' having evaporated, the 'solution' does likewise. But it does not follow that for the unenlightened the discipline of transcendence is unnecessary, or that because we are, in truth, already free, nothing need be done except acknowledge the fact intellectually and carry on in our old unenlightened ways. The enlightened individual is not merely a spiritually energized ego; in the realized state there is no greater sense of identification with the notion of 'self' than there is with the notion of an object, or another. Nor is *nirvana* merely feeling good in the waking state, and to say or act as if it were is to misrepresent Truth by interpreting it on the level of conventional and unenlightened experience, a trap into which more than one popularizer of the Buddhist way in the past few years has fallen.

The intellectual and doctrinal expansion of the Mahayana was mirrored in its art and architecture. Once the restrictions of the original teaching had been expanded, it was as if the irrepressible fecundity of the Indian imagination was freed to express itself in sublime cosmologies and panoramic celestial vistas, many of them drawing inspiration from the cultural matrix of Vedic Hinduism from which Buddhism had originally sprung. In a burst of creative energy fed by intense mystical and visionary experience, transcendental pantheons of celestial buddhas, *bodhisattvas* and divine beings inhabiting other-worldly realms were cognized and represented in order to stimulate devotion, faith and contemplation. Wherever the Mahayana spread, these pantheons appear in various forms, often incorporating local deities and cults into their rich array. The whole was underpinned by sublime and subtle metaphysical systems that mocked the common-sense laws of time and space. More than one contemporary writer has pointed out striking affinities between the Mahayana world-view and the realities postulated at the far reaches of modern scientific knowledge, the Alice-in-Wonderland world of quantum physics.

The Spread of the Dharma

Having taken firm root in India, the teachings of Shakyamuni spread rapidly eastwards to all parts of Asia. The Theravada travelled south to Sri Lanka and thence to Burma, Thailand and Indo-China, whereas the Mahayana took a

Chenrezi (Sanskrit: Avalokiteshvara), bodhisattva of compassion. Tibet, 18th century.

northern route, to the Himalayas and Tibet, and on to Mongolia, China and Japan. Many countries supported both Theravada and Mahayana sects, concurrently or sequentially. Throughout its spread, Buddhism, like any other colonizing religion, assumed different forms according to the geographical, social and cultural conditions it encountered. The result is a tree of rich and immensely varied foliage. In lush Sri Lanka, the first country outside India to receive Buddhist missionaries, a gentle and reclusive Theravada doctrine emphasizing ethical conduct and strict mental training flourished among the incorrigible green of that island. At the other extreme, in the high altitude desert plateau of Tibet, influenced by landscapes of a lunar strangeness and the indigenous steppe culture that practised arcane shamanistic techniques of ecstasy, sacrifice and oracular trance, schools evolved with a fantastic and baroque cosmology replete with peaceful and wrathful deities, ritual objects made from human bones, and complex recondite litanies devoted to the summoning, appeasing or banishing of raw elemental energies. This esoteric branch of the Mahayana is known as the Vajrayana: 'The Way of the Adamantine Thunderbolt'.

The Way of Tolerance

What is so extraordinary from the point of view of the history of religions is that the spread of Buddhism was totally peaceful. The *dharma* first received state patronage in the third century BC under the Mauryan Emperor Ashoka, who adopted it after being disgusted by a particularly bloody military campaign in Orissa. With the fervour of the newly converted, he had his new faith spread rapidly throughout much of northern India and Pakistan. Some of the earliest Buddhist archaeological remains date from this time: the famous Ashokan columns – pillars etched with quotes from the texts and directions to fellow-Buddhists – and rocks carved with inscriptions in a similar vein. One of these well conveys the mood of serene tolerance that informed the propagation:

> One should not honour only one's own religion and condemn the religions of others, but one should honour others' religions for this or that reason. . . . In acting otherwise one digs the grave of one's own religion and also does harm to other religions. Whosoever honours his own religion and condemns other religions does so, indeed, through devotion to his own religion, thinking: 'I will glorify my own religion.' But on the contrary, in so doing he injures his own religion more gravely. So concord is good: let all listen, and be willing to listen to the doctrines professed by others. (*Ashokan Rock Edict No.12*)

It is this type of intelligent openness that, over the last century or so, has attracted increasing numbers of Westerners, some of whom admit to being tired of a narrowness within their inherited tradition which claims to have a monopoly on the truth. Though Buddhism has been, since its beginnings, a proselytizing religion, it has never shed blood in its desire to convert. Non-violence is a cardinal tenet of the faith, the practical outcome of a loving-kindness extended not only to humans but to 'all sentient beings'. The

A Zen monk in meditation. Japan, 17th century.

Dhammapada explains this attitude of non-violence with a simplicity that is as forceful as it is endearing:

> All beings tremble before danger, all fear death. When a man considers this, he does not kill or cause to kill. All beings fear before danger, life is dear to all. When a man considers this, he does not kill or cause to kill.

There has never been a Buddhist inquisition or holy war, nor indeed any rigorous and punitive attempts to stamp out 'heresy'. Buddhism does not value mere belief, let alone acquiescence based on fear, nor has it ever promoted a doctrine of an individual 'soul' which must be 'saved' at all costs – including, if necessary, the destruction of the body. While disagreement between the Mahayana and Theravada schools was often keen, it was always peaceful, as evinced by the medieval university of Nalanda in Bihar, where over ten thousand monks of different sects lived, studied, meditated and debated together in perfect harmony, until the place was razed by the invading Muslims. The *dharma*, as natural law, is able to accommodate and support an enormous variety of perspectives, opinions and beliefs, each more or less useful at its own time as a provisional step on the path of clearer understanding. This variety increased as the Mahayana expanded until, in Tibet, it was said that 'every lama has his own religion'.

To the Buddhist, the idea of coercing anyone to accept a complete body of beliefs all at once, before this brief life-span dissolves into an eternity of damnation or salvation, is erroneously based on a naively simplistic view of time and the very nature of things. The unfolding of the historical process through linear time, as the expression of an exclusive covenant with a parent deity figure – the mainstays of the orthodox Judeo-Christian view – may well have been a sustaining or advantageous tribal myth but, in Buddhist eyes, it does scant justice to the extraordinarily rich and complex realities of cosmic life. This, as the Mahayana delighted in showing, evolves through countless cycles, in countless universes, through countless aeons of time, in countless forms. To limit the irruption of Truth to one particular place, time, culture or creed is as futile as trying to 'grasp the air in a pair of fire-tongs'.

Another factor in determining the Buddhist record of tolerance was socio-political as much as doctrinal. The monastic basis of the reclusive *sangha* mitigated the political involvement that is inextricably part of any religious fundamentalism, and this happily helped Buddhism keep clear of violent conflicts of doctrinal self-interest. Nor have the followers of the Buddhist way ever indulged in the sort of missionary work which has played so shameful a part in the historical spread of Christianity, and which, even today, is resulting in cultural holocausts in remote parts of South America and New Guinea. Perhaps the emphasis on contemplative disciplines and self-knowledge that preoccupies practising Buddhists reduces the likelihood of personal fantasies emerging to become projected or glorified as directions from some divine being. In their analysis and evaluation of the human personality and its hidden reaches, the approach of most schools of Buddhism is more akin to modern psychology than to traditional religion. Indeed, it is the sophistication and acuity of its psychological analysis that makes the *dharma* appear relevant to increasing numbers of people in the secularized modern world.

Nevertheless, though the Buddhist record in matters of doctrinal chauvinism remains relatively unstained, it would be naive to suppose that professed Buddhists have always existed entirely aloof from violence and conflict. The Buddhist kings of Burma, most notably Anuruddha in the eleventh century, conducted many devastating raids into neighbouring lands in a ruthless search for scriptures and valuable images, sacking whatever lay in their path, including numerous temples and holy sites. The Buddhist kingdoms of Burma, Thailand and Cambodia have engaged in many mutually destructive wars over the centuries, and in the seventeenth century the Tibetan Gelugpa (Yellow Hat) school, of which the Dalai Lama is the reincarnating leader, joined forces with the Mongol warlords to establish their supremacy over the rival Nyingma (Red Hat) sects, with many of the remote monasteries having their own armies of soldier-monks. Similarly, many of the warring factions that split medieval China and Japan were ostensibly Buddhist. Though these last examples can legitimately be seen as more the result of Mongol militarism than religious zeal, the fact remains that Buddhism, like any other religion, has at times been used to cloak military ambition, and as an excuse to pursue ancient racial, territorial and politico-economic conflicts. In the context of twentieth-century secularism, nationalistic sentiments have not infrequently been sanctified with quasi-Buddhist justification, as in the Boxer Rebellion in China in the 1920s, and the Independence Movement in Burma a decade or so later. In recent times Vietnam, Tibet, Sri Lanka and Burma have all seen their Buddhist monks join popular uprisings against oppression.

Buddhism Today

As a vital and flexible body of knowledge and practice, the *dharma* has always adapted to the various situations in which it has found itself. This adaptability is no less evident today when the teachings of the Buddha are increasingly propagated in both East and West, under both free market and socialist systems. In its homeland India, the Buddha's message was almost unheard for a thousand years after the devastating Islamic invasions that began in earnest in the twelfth century AD. In recent years, however, large numbers from the lower and scheduled castes have converted to the teachings of Shakyamuni as an escape from a social system they feel has little to offer them. In this they are following the example of Dr Ambedakar, the lawyer who framed the Indian Constitution in 1947 by which discrimination on the grounds of caste was made illegal. An 'untouchable' himself, he adopted Buddhism which he saw as a fairer way ahead for the newly independent subcontinent.

In Thailand, where a highly refined culture has been nourished by the teachings of the Buddha for over two thousand years, the years since the American involvement in Vietnam have seen a steady erosion of traditional values under Western influences. As a response to what many Thais see as a prostitution of the Thai way of life, several new Buddhist organizations have arisen. The most influential of these is the Dhammakaya Temple, a highly organized body devoted to nothing less than the complete moral regeneration of the country. The Temple is unusual in that it appeals mainly to middle class and university-educated Thais, and concentrating its campaigns on the institutes of higher education, draws several thousands to its weekly meditation meetings and its two-month Mass Ordination Course each summer. The clearest political statement of this reforming mood is the Palang Dharma (Forces of Spiritual Justice) Party, led by the hugely popular Governor of Bangkok, Chamlong Srimuang, himself a devout Buddhist who according to all reports lives a life of great simplicity. Further east in Japan, Nichiren Buddhism, of which the lay organization is called the Soka Gakkai, is the fastest growing religious organization in Japan, and is said to have more followers in the West than all the other forms of Buddhism combined. Well-established in the Japanese corporate world, the Soka Gakkai has enormous financial interests.

Tibet, brutalized over the last forty years by the occupation of the Chinese Communists, has suffered enormously from the vagaries of twentieth-century international politics. However, despite the Chinese attempt to destroy completely all traces of Tibetan culture, those Tibetans who remain in their country cling tenaciously to the tattered and bleeding remnants of their faith. Many have become refugees, including their leader in exile, His Holiness the Dalai Lama, whom Tibetans consider to be the incarnation of Chenrezi, the Mahayana *bodhisattva* of Compassion. Despite being spurned by many Western heads of governments anxious not to lose prospective commercial advantages from the Chinese, he emerged during the 1980s as a world figure of considerable spiritual stature and a symbol inspiring many who are working for change on a variety of fronts: human rights, ecology and so on. Awarded the Nobel Peace Prize in 1989, His Holiness's compassion, patience and loving-kindness towards the oppressors of his country and culture, and those who, by their silence, tacitly condone it, are an extraordinary tribute to, and example of, the Buddhist way.

It was these waves of refugees who first initiated the considerable current interest in Tibetan Buddhism. Since the late 1960s many high lamas have visited, taught and settled in both Europe and America, establishing communities of followers. One of the most influential of these was the late Chogyam Trungpa Rinpoche, whose continuing gift to the West lies in his modification of traditional Buddhist practice and his introduction of a largely demythologized and psychological interpretation of the Tibetan perspective to suit the needs of contemporary society, especially North America. Largely due to Trungpa's work, the vibrantly powerful Vajrayana iconography has been applied beyond the boundaries of Tibetan culture, to serve as a vehicle for expressing insights gleaned from psychotherapy. Thus some of the most recondite aspects of Buddhism have entered the vocabulary of modern Western therapists who use, for example, the Tibetan images of 'wrathful deities' as a means of acknowledging, accepting and transmuting the sort of negative emotions – anger, resentment, jealousy and so on – that have traditionally been repressed or denied validity in Western religion. One such therapist is Tsultrim Allione, who having been recognized by the Karmapa as an associate from a previous incarnation, was ordained as a nun in the Kagyu lineage. Now living back in the world, she works in New York using a combination of mask-drama, role play and Vajrayana insights to express her own brand of feminist and psychotherapeutic teachings which she calls, after the Tibetan female deities, *dakini* wisdom.

For the first time in history, Tibetan *tulkus* are now reincarnating in the West. The first European-born lama was born in 1985 as Osel Torres, the son of a Spanish Buddhist couple living in a mountain village in Granada. The baby Osel was soon recognized by various high lamas including the Dalai Lama as the reincarnation of Thubten Yeshe, a *tulku* who had done much to spread the *dharma* in the West, dying in San Francisco in 1984. Osel is now in Nepal, receiving the full monastic education accorded to one of his status. His mother is making no predictions for the future. As she says:

> What will happen remains to be seen. I expect Osel will spend half his time in the East and half in the West. After all he is a mixture of the two. As well as Buddhism he will also get a foundation in Christianity, and an American disciple has already opened a bank account for his Harvard education. If Buddhism is to have any meaning in the West, we must extract its essence, then build our own culture around it. That was Lama Yeshe's vision. And that, perhaps, is what Osel will achieve.

Buddhism is flourishing throughout North America, the country in which Buddhist teachings first began to reach a widespread Western audience through the avant-garde literary scene of the late 1950s and early 1960s, with writers such as Gary Snyder, Jack Kerouac, Paul Reps and Alan Watts. At the opposite end of the spectrum from the Vajrayana teachers is the Vietnamese monk Thich Nhat Hanh whose simple everyday presentation of the Theravadin teachings has captured the imagination of Americans from all walks of life. Once nominated by Martin Luther King for the Nobel Peace Prize, he is a prolific speaker and writer and a tireless campaigner on behalf of the Vietnamese boat people. Recently, Thich Nhat Hanh has devoted much of his time to applying the balm of the Buddha's teaching to the psychologically damaged veterans of the Vietnam War.

Kwan-yin, bodhisattva of compassion. China, 13th century.

Britain, like most European countries, has many *dharma* centres, serving both expatriate Buddhists and native converts. A Japanese peace pagoda overlooks the river Thames from Battersea Park in the heart of London, while in the quintessentially English hamlet of Chithurst in Hampshire, a group of American and European monks, followers of the Thai teacher Ajahn Chah, live a life as close to the original message of the Buddha as possible. Early each morning, before even the village postman and milkman deliver, the monks are out barefoot, walking the lanes on the traditional alms-round.

The Dharma and the New Age

The last few years have witnessed an explosion of interest in the various departments of the spiritual supermarket. Ancient and traditional teachings are cobbled together in ever more exotic combinations to console the ant-like scurry of our anxious lives and the resulting packages are disseminated in ever more efficient and profitable ways around the humming global networks. Such a flurry of excitement in the supernatural is partly a sign of the times; as we approach the end of the millennium Western civilization is undergoing dramatic change, and the declining years of the great ages of Greece and Rome witnessed comparable enthusiasms. But while the increasing interest in Buddhism may appear to be just a part of the 'New Age', it is well to remember that the inner life is vulgarized at its peril. New Age courses and techniques promising instant enlightenment abound, and in the name of Higher Wisdom all sorts of experiences are manipulated or encouraged. Truth, however, cannot be reduced to mere information or mere experience to be accumulated by the seeker as yet another form of mass-consumerism. If this happens, a subtle form of self-aggrandizement can ensue. No egocentric experience, no matter how consoling, brings Enlightenment, for Enlightenment is precisely the effortless transcendence of the egotistical perspective which is, by its very nature, constantly seeking ever more alluring experiences. While it is true that many of the concerns of Buddhism are shared by the apostles of the New Age, it should not be forgotten that a mature sense of discrimination is always an important aspect of true Buddhist practice. Without such discrimination (symbolized by the razor-sharp sword of Manjushri in Vajrayana iconography) it is easy to get caught up in the trappings of spiritual materialism. Unconscious fantasies may be indulged and glorified as directions from some exotic 'spirit guide' who advises on what stocks and shares to buy, or what colour would be most spiritually auspicious for the new car. Or in the widespread discussion of past lives, nearly everyone seems to remember being Cleopatra or Napoleon, or some high priest from Atlantis. Such glamorous conditions may or may not be true – after all, as the Mahayana delights in showing, the universe contains infinite possibilities – the more relevant question from the Buddhist point of view is this: are they conducive to wisdom and compassion? If not, they are on the same level as TV evangelism in their exploitation of mass credulity and uninspected emotionalism.

For those who tread the Buddhist path, life becomes endowed with a profound simplicity, an ordinariness that is simultaneously a continuing revelation.

> And why? Because it is perfect wisdom which appeases all evil and does not increase it, beginning with ordinary greed up to the attempt to seize on *nirvana* as one's own personal property. And the Gods and all the Buddhas, and all the *bodhisattvas* will protect this follower of perfect wisdom. And this will be an advantage even here and now. (*The Perfection of Wisdom*)

The Future

From its beginnings Buddhism was a monastic religion, and an ascetic bias is always discernible in the original texts. The Buddha was born a prince, and was in a position to renounce the material advantages that most of us spend most of our lives struggling to acquire. It is also true that one becomes good at what one practises, and normal worldly life leaves little time to focus in any sustained way on the meditative disciplines that are the nourishing heart of the Buddhist endeavour. However, the practice of Buddhism is not confined to renunciates, and many millions of normal householders are following the Buddha's path today. The 'great renunciation' is not a pattern to be emulated literally, but can be seen as a metaphor for the willingness to leave behind old patterns of thought and behaviour and set out on a voyage of discovery about oneself and the world. Nevertheless, a life that is expressive of the profound commitment to realize Truth is another order of existence to the life of the normal social personality. Indeed not only is it probably uninteresting to such a person, but may even arouse in him or her defensive reactions of hostility or cynicism, just those feelings, in fact, that are commonly directed towards the contemplative life in the contemporary climate of scientific materialism.

In the weeks following the Enlightenment the Buddha was reluctant to teach at all, convinced that the truth of *nirvana* was too profound to be grasped by most people. He referred to the *dharma* as being *patisotagami*: 'going against the grain', by which he meant that in employing the reversal of attention to reveal the subjective basis of all we normally consider 'objective', it questions many of our basic assumptions about life and its purpose. In so doing, it is liable to 'rub people up the wrong way' and expose our resistances to change and growth.

Happily, many of the prejudices that have in the past militated against a sympathetic consideration of Buddhism are today being swept away by global changes invested with the irresistible force of evolution. The modern secular age, born with the Reformation, has thrived on the doctrine of individuality, from which have come the democratic and capitalistic systems, and the scientific and technological revolutions. But true individuality is not the isolated ego, fearfully struggling for survival against all others and divorced from the nourishment and morality that springs from the intuitive realization of the subtle interconnectedness of all life.

Whatever benefits scientific secularism has had in improving the material conditions of life, one price paid for this mechanistic bias has been that the potential of the human being was overlooked in favour of what is obvious, visible or quantifiable. Humanity's greatest untapped resource, its own consciousness, has been largely ignored, and with it the possibility of levels of reality not vested solely in the objective realm accessible to gross sensory experience. Mere manipulation and rearrangement of the outer order – political, social, economic – can no longer be seen as the only solution.

The devotees of scientism, the irrational belief in continual progress through the application of scientific materialism, are increasingly being faced with the evidence that their approach on its own, unnurtured by subjective values, does not work. It is no coincidence that the societies most entranced by scientism are those which, despite their material affluence, most glaringly display the symptoms of a deep spiritual malaise. Anxiety, greed and violence are no less evident in the technologically sophisticated cultures precisely because there is more to life than increasing its efficiency. One does not need to look far to see that the Tree of Life is dying, and Mother Earth has cancer of the womb.

And yet, on the other side there is a tremendous upsurge of positive and creative response to the current dilemma, for awareness brings its own action. The growth of interest in Buddhism is part of a world-wide paradigm shift, a change of attitudes found in all spheres – medical, ecological, spiritual – that is pointing towards a new and greatly expanded vision of human possibilities. This vision leads inexorably in the direction of greater freedom, profounder understanding and more awesome responsibility. To date our global culture has, for the large part, been fashioned by perspectives belonging to only the first two stages of mankind: childhood, characterized by dependence, and adolescence, characterized by the reaction into 'independence'. What lies ahead is the third and most challenging stage – adulthood. True adulthood is characterized by self-transcendence, and this is the way of the Buddha.

The walking Buddha. Thailand, 14th–15th century.

Buddhism teaches that the way to
Truth is a journey inwards; all of us
possess the Buddha nature deep
within, beyond the threshold of the
various levels of our social
personality. Images are often set at
the cardinal and mid-points of a
building, whether temple or stupa,
serving both to draw the
worshipper inwards to the centre of
the shrine, and at the same time to
radiate the sacred inner influence
of the structure outwards to all
directions of the universe. The
decoration of the arches in this
Burmese pagoda was derived from
Sri Lanka, and was later to
influence the embellishment of Thai
architecture. (Pagan, Burma, 12th
century)

As the spiritual centre of consciousness, the head received particular attention from Buddhist artists. Here the dreamy head of a stucco Buddha (*right*) from Gandhara, the origin of the earliest school of representation, shows the influence of Greece in its similarity to the adolescent Apollonian sun-god of late Hellenistic art. Two of the thirty-two bodily signs (*lakshana*) of a Buddha are discernible: the third eye (*urna*) in the centre of the forehead, signifying spiritual insight, and the protuberance at the crown (*ushnisha*), which represents Enlightenment, when the 'thousand-petalled lotus' at the apex of the subtle body is fully opened. More typically oriental in their willowy stylization are the two heads of the *bodhisattva* Miroku (the Japanese Maitreya), the Buddha of the future age, shown pondering the means to achieve the salvation of humanity. Both are in wood and show a third *lakshana*, the elongated ear lobes which, although originally perhaps caused by Gautama's princely earrings, came to be a symbol of wisdom. (*Below:* Koryuji Temple, Kyoto, mid-7th century; *left:* Chuguji Convent, Nara, 7th century; *right:* Hadda, Afghanistan, c. 1st century AD)

Pilgrimage to holy places has always been an important part of Buddhist worship, and enormous images were often set at particularly striking or inaccessible places along the route or carved out of the living rock, as in this example from Tibet (*left*). Of the

three most common positions — sitting, standing and reclining — the latter (which technically refers to the death of the Buddha) lent itself to large-scale representation and was especially popular in Sri Lanka and South-East Asia. This one (*below*) is over 14 metres (45 feet) long. Spiritual power is expressed not only by size but also by accumulation: groups of Buddha figures in different positions were not uncommon. Originally protected by structures of brick or wood which have since disappeared, they are now exposed to the elements, often scattered amidst the ruins of ancient cities, which add to their dramatic force. (*Left:* On the road to the Valley of Kings, Tibet; *below left:* Kamphang Phet, Thailand, 14th century; *below:* Polonnaruwa, Sri Lanka, mid-12th century)

Buddhist iconographers, like all craftsmen of the sacred, employed a limited stylistic vocabulary, producing variations on a relatively small number of forms. This conservatism suits the essentially didactic aim of sacred art: repetition inculcates the message and adds a cumulative power that stretches across different cultures.

The Buddha (*left*) is from Thailand, but shows strong Cambodian influence in both the facial features and the regal attire, while the shape of the *ushnisha* (the protuberance at the crown) is mirrored by the Burmese-style stupa behind. Borobodur, the largest Buddhist shrine in the world, forms an enormous three-dimensional map of the cosmos. On its many terraces, dozens of miniature stupas contain a Buddha figure, a combination symbolizing simultaneously the various celestial levels of creation and the innate Buddha nature within us all. (*Left:* Ayutthaya, Thailand, late 15th century; *above:* Borobodur, central Java, mid-8th century)

Initially rainy-season retreats for the itinerant monks, rock-cut sanctuaries became the first permanent homes of the monastic communities. Often set near the junction of trade routes, they also served as shrines for pilgrims and merchants, on whom the monks largely depended for their livelihood. Simple to maintain, cool in summer and warm in winter, they persisted long after the ability to build free-standing structures was developed. An architecture of mass, burrowed out of the living rock, they were symbolically suited to the introspection practised by the meditative recluse. Like the labyrinths of Western mythology, their thresholds were often protected by fierce guardian creatures who dispelled the powers of negativity. (*Left:* Yungang Caves, northern China, *c.* 5th century; *above:* Temple guardian, Kathmandu, *c.* 12th century)

Constructed according to the laws of sacred proportion, each Buddha image should be consecrated and empowered by specific rituals before it is 'alive' enough to be worshipped. The same image serves different purposes. At the most popular level it is considered the repository of supernatural power, recipient of prayers, and a magical being that can intercede in daily life. In the resolutely animistic countries of South-East Asia, images often have distinct personalities and preferences, and are sometimes even jealous of each other. At another level, the image is a springboard for meditation, a means of filling the mind with a form which represents perfection. True appreciation of form leads to the formless, just as true perception of sound leads to silence. (*Left:* The Buddha in 'Earth-touching posture', the gesture that finally defeated the forces of ignorance and grounded his Enlightenment, Pagan, Burma, 19th century; *right:* Monk in meditation, Bangkok, Thailand)

Graceful attenuation of form is the hallmark of the Thai aesthetic sense, and some of the most beautiful Buddhist art was produced in Thailand. The high-point of Thai artistic endeavour was the school of Sukhothai, the first capital of the united Thai nation, that had at its centre Wat Mahathat (*above*), photographed here during Loy Kratong, the Festival of Lights celebrated each November. South-East Asia was known in antiquity as Suvarnabhumi, the Land of Gold, and in Thailand gold, traditionally provided by Chinese merchants, has always been used extensively to fashion and adorn images. Quite apart from its commercial value, gold is the material that best suggests the celestial perception of Enlightenment. The Buddha image (*right*) is in the meditation posture, surmounted by the parasol which alludes both to the Buddha's royal status and the bodhi tree under which he attained *nirvana*. (*Above*: Wat Mahathat, Sukhothai, Thailand, 14th century; *right*: Buddha, Wat Po, Bangkok)

One of the most celebrated miracles of the Buddha occurred when, to confound a group of heretics at a town called Shravasti, he multiplied himself into a thousand Buddhas, each seated on a lotus throne. The theme was seized on with delight by the Mahayana painters and sculptors in particular, who used it to cover cave and monastery walls. Such profuse illustrations refer not only to the actual miracle, but also to the celestial hierarchies that celebrate the universality of Shakyamuni's teaching through all

time and space. The solidity of rock
adds to the sense of the utter
invincibility of the *dharma*, and
lends dramatic acoustic effect to
the sonorous chanting of the
monks, while the darkened interiors
glow with the fugitive and
unearthly light of candles and oil
lamps. (*Left:* Part of the Rock of a
Thousand Buddhas, Lung-Men,
northern China, 6th century; *right:*
Interior of a cave at Yun-Kang,
northern China, mid-5th century,
with the Buddha in the unusual
'European' position, making the
'Fear not' *mudra*)

The cave art of India, especially that of Ajanta (left), inspired in turn the Buddhist painting of Bihar, Bengal, Nepal, and Tibet. A favourite subject was the Jataka Tales, folk stories of the Buddha's previous incarnations as a human or an animal. This Jataka scene depicts Shakyamuni as the Prince Mahajanaka, who, even as he is receiving lustration as the crown prince, vows to renounce the world. The murals, burnished with shells or stones, glowingly depict the richness of a refined and aristocratic sensibility, and date from the Gupta period, the golden age of Buddhist civilization in India. Many of the scenes, set in luxuriant and courtly surroundings, provide rare and valuable records of contemporary dress and architecture. (Left: Scene from the Mahajanaka Jataka, Cave no.1, Ajanta, India, 5th century; above: Celestial maiden from the Lion Rock cave, Sigiriya, Sri Lanka, late 5th century)

In Buddhist iconography, all hand gestures (*mudras*) have a meaning, just as they do in Hindu images. *Mudra* movements mirror the movements of the mind, and are one of the main symbolic means of conveying the principles of the *dharma*. One of the most common is the *mudra* of teaching (*left*), in which the fine discriminative insight of the Buddhist way is portrayed by the joining of the thumb and index finger, a circularity also recalling the Wheel of the Law and the eternal continuation of the *dharma*. Less usual is the healing *mudra* from a bronze image of Yakushi (*right*), the Japanese Buddha known as the Master of Medicine, who cures the root disease of ignorance. In his palm is the *lakshana* of the 'lotus whorl' in the form of the eight-spoked Wheel of the Law. *Mudras* may well have originated in the ancient gestures of Indian dance, such as this representation of the lotus (*below left*), symbol of purity and Enlightenment. (*Right:* Detail of Buddha image in Yakushi-ji temple, Japan; *above left:* Detail of Yakushi, Japan, 7th century; *below left:* The *padma mudra* from Bharata Natyam, the oldest school of Indian classical dance)

When Buddhism reached the Himalayas in the 8th century AD it inherited Bon-po, the indigenous shamanistic culture, in which elemental energies are summoned and appeased in a world that is unpredictable and always potentially hostile. This world-view, found in various forms all over Central Asia, was heavily to influence Vajrayana, the type of Buddhism found in Tibet, Ladakh, Mongolia, Bhutan, Sikkim and parts of Nepal. Prayer flags (*left*), block-printed with passages from the scriptures, send supplications up to the heavens, while a wayside protector (*above*) displays the open mouth, protruding fangs and pop eyes that characterize a deity awaiting sacrifice. (*Left:* Travellers resting on the road to Thimpu, Bhutan; *above:* Mountain shrine, Ladakh)

53

Feet represent the grounding of the transcendent, and have long been the focus of respect in India. The 'lotus feet' of gods and gurus are worshipped there even today, elders and parents merit having their feet touched in respect by their children, and bare feet are always expected in temples, shrines

and houses. In the early days of Buddhism, natural declivities were sometimes seen as evidence of the Buddha's footprint (*buddhapada*), and especially in Theravada countries the cult flourished as a natural extension of animistic stone worship. This example (*left*) shows a catholic combination of Hindu and Buddhist symbols: the solar disc, related to the deity Vishnu (of whom orthodox Hindus see Shakyamuni as the ninth incarnation), the trident of Shiva, representing the unity of past, present and future, and the eight-fold lotus, alluding to Enlightenment and the path there.

The soles of the reclining Buddha (*above*) are covered with the 108 auspicious signs of the faith. (*Above left: Buddhapada* from Takht-i-Bahi, Pakistan, 1st century BC; *left: Buddhapada* from Bodh Gaya, Bihar, scene of the Buddha's *nirvana*; *above:* Reclining Buddha, Kyauk Htat, Gyi Pagoda, Rangoon, Burma)

Buddhism relies on the ancient arrangement, little understood in modern society, whereby the monks provide spiritual teaching, education and disinterested advice, and the lay population provides material support. The giving of alms and the offering of help in the monastery are seen as direct and practical ways through which the average person can foster the selfless virtues of generosity and service and also gain merit for

future incarnations. In countries like Thailand and Burma, the early morning alms-round, with the monks barefoot and dressed in the traditional saffron of renunciation, is still very much part of the daily routine. (*Left:* Novices in Mae Hong Son, north-west Thailand; *below*: Manuscript illumination showing donation scenes, Burma, 19th century; *right:* Monks outside the Emerald Buddha Temple, Bangkok, Thailand)

The Japanese school of Zen, a mixture of Buddhist meditative philosophy pared down to its essentials and the nature mysticism of Taoism, came from China to Japan. In Zen, the arts are seen as extensions of nature's spontaneous perfection into the realm of human affairs, an expression normally blocked by the rational mind. This emphasis on the natural led in time to an iconoclastic irreverence, fuelled by disinclination to conform to medieval Japan's hieratic society. The eternal perfection of nature is here expressed by the circle (*above*), a mandala of essential simplicity and symbol of wholeness, whose inscription reads: 'The spirit of Zen is everywhere', and by the timeless tranquillity of the rock garden. (*Above:* Brush and ink drawing, Japan, 19th century; *left:* The 'Moon door' of a monastery, Wu-Shi, China; *right:* The Nanzenji temple, Kyoto, Japan)

The entire universe is ultimately
nothing but light, in different
densities and gradations. Thus light
is an important symbol of reality in
Buddhism, and is always one of the
principal offerings made to a shrine
or image. In Thai temples (*right*) an
orange candle, signifying the
individual consciousness of the
worshipper, is offered with flowers
representing the senses and three
sticks of sandalwood incense that
allude to the 'Three Jewels' of
Buddhism: the Buddha, the *dharma*,
and the *sangha*. In Tibet (*above*)
where life is very hard, the lamps
are fuelled by valuable butter made
from the milk of the yak, the
Tibetans' most precious animal,
whereas the evening ceremony at
one of the sixty temples on the
'Nine Flower Mountain' relies more
prosaically on hurricane lamps.
(*Left:* Interior of Jiahua Shan temple,
China; *above:* Pilgrim inside the
Jokhang, Lhasa, Tibet; *right:*
Worshipper at Wat Phra Keoh,
Bangkok, Thailand)

That Enlightenment is a state of effortless being (*sahaja*) is mirrored in the graceful ease of most Buddhist images, whose limbs often seem to have the luxuriance of a sap-filled plant. The origin of this aesthetic is to be found partly in the natural grace of the people of southern and South-East Asia, and partly in ideals of beauty that hark back originally to India. These teach that the bodies of gods and teachers should be shown to radiate *prāna*, the subtle life energy which flows unobstructed in the wise. The result is a sensualized spirituality infusing a dreamlike plasticity of form. This effect, achieved in media as different as bronze (*right*) and lacquered papier-mâché (*bottom left*), is quite different from the realistic musculature of the Western classical tradition. (*Above:* Monk reading paper, Rangoon, Burma; *left:* Listening disciple, Burma, 19th century; *right: Bodhisattva* in the posture of Royal Ease, Sri Lanka, 11th century)

Treading the Buddhist path is an everyday affair, step by step towards the light. (Early morning alms-round, Wat Mahathat, Bangkok, Thailand)

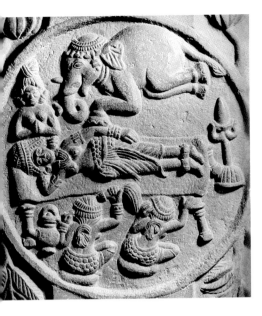

The Journey to Liberation

The story of the Buddha's birth is a version of the 'divine child' myth: his mother, Queen Maya (*maya* is a Sanskrit word used to describe the universe as a magical and illusory show) dreams that an auspicious white elephant bearing a lotus in its trunk enters her side. Royal astrologers at the court of Kapilavastu interpret the dream to mean that she has conceived a being that will be a great leader, either of the spiritual or the temporal realm. (*Above*: Queen Maya's dream, sandstone, Bharut, India, 2nd century)

She gives birth effortlessly, supported on a tree like a nature spirit, to a baby that emerges from her side. The infant Gautama takes seven steps: each time his foot touches the ground a lotus springs up, symbolizing the seven *chakras* (energy centres) that are naturally open in Enlightenment, and he announces this to be his last incarnation.

The more time elapsed after the Buddha's death, the more his legend grew, drawing on archaic and often universal motifs long established in the Indian folk memory. The second stage in the hero myth involves a symbolic death: withdrawal from the familiar world, and a period of solitary introspection followed by an eventual return, transfigured, to engage anew in everyday life. After marrying and having a son, Gautama encounters the 'Three Marks of Impermanence' (old age, illness and death), and decides to leave his family and renounce his throne. (*Left*: Birth, and first steps of Gautama, murals, Manjushri Temple, Alchi, Ladakh, 12th century; *bottom left*: Leaving the palace, Burmese manuscript, 19th century)

His abandonment of sensual life is symbolized by the cutting of his hair, and he undertakes a life of rigorous austerity. Unsatisfied by the extremes of luxury on the one hand and self-denial on the other, he realizes the wisdom of the Middle Way of

moderation, and vows not to leave the bodhi tree in the garden at Bodh Gaya until he has attained liberation. Through meditation he eventually transcends the subconscious tendencies of fear and limitation – the binding forces of ignorance – that are symbolized as the army of Mara, the Tempter, and attains perfect Enlightenment. Challenged by Mara as to the stability of his state, the Buddha calls the Mother Earth to be his witness, touching the ground in front of him, a gesture that also signifies the grounding

of absolute knowledge. For those treading the Path, the journey of withdrawal, apotheosis and return is re-enacted on a personal level through the daily practice of meditation. (*Top left*: Gilt terracotta statue, Pagan, Burma, 11th century; *top right*: Gandhara statue, Pakistan, 2nd century BC; *above*: Mara's army, gateway detail from the Great Stupa, Sanchi, India, 1st century BC; *left*: The Lion Lord, Wat Phra Singh, Chiang Mai, Thailand, 14th century)

The Enlightened Life

The Buddha was often shown surmounted by the sacred serpent-king (*nagaraja*) Muchalinda, who sheltered him from a storm in the garden at Bodh Gaya. The synoptic nature of sacred images aligns the serpent with the royal parasol, symbol of Gautama's royal status, and the tree under which he attained liberation. Now a living Tree of Life, the bodhi tree is worshipped by his followers, among whom are monkeys, which in Buddhist iconography represent the restlessly chattering mind finally conquered by wisdom. (*Left*: Statue, Cambodia, 12th century; *above*: Gateway detail, the Great Stupa, Sanchi, India, 1st century BC; *below left*: The Buddha surrounded by monks, Peshawar, Pakistan, 2nd century; *below*: King Suddhodana, the Buddha's father, feeding a monk, Burma, 19th century)

The symbolism of the seven-headed serpent Muchalinda alludes to the rising of the *kundalini* energy through the seven *chakras*, or energy centres, of the subtle body, and the opening of the 'thousand-petalled lotus' *chakra* above the crown of the head, while the storm at Bodh Gaya represents the final psychic upheaval that precedes Enlightenment. Word of an enlightened teacher spreads rapidly; the Buddha founds the 'company of the good' (*sangha*), and the lifestyle of the itinerant order of mendicants is established.

Queen Maya had died shortly after Gautama's birth, and the Buddha spends three months preaching to her in the Tavatimsa heaven. This myth is the origin of the annual custom of the three-month rainy-season retreat. The incident also inspired representations of Shakyamuni in the standing and walking poses, though the latter was only really developed in Thai art. The Buddha spends an energetic forty years travelling around north-east India, founding orders of monks and nuns and groups of laymen and laywomen, teaching, debating, refuting heretics and performing miracles, at one time transforming himself into a thousand Buddhas. Then, at the age of eighty, attended by his followers and his favourite disciple, Ananda ('The Joyous'), he reaches the outskirts of the town of Kushinagara, where illness compels him to stop in the forest of Uparavarta. Here, reclining between two trees, he calls his followers together, and after offering to answer any questions they might have and counselling the assembled company to work towards their own Enlightenment, he leaves the body. The death (*mahaparinirvana*) of Shakyamuni is the textual origin of all the reclining Buddha images. (*Above left*: The Buddha descending from the Tavatimsa heaven, mural, Thailand; *above right*: The miracle of the thousand Buddhas, mural, Manjushri Temple, Alchi, Ladakh, 12th century; *below*: The death of the Buddha, rock carving, Cave no. 26, Ajanta, India, 6th century)

The Growth of the Image

In Buddhism, as in Christianity, it was three or four hundred years after the death of the founder of the faith that the first figurative images appeared, perhaps as a response to fading memories of the early days of the community. The first cult objects were the flywhisk or parasol – symbols of Gautama's royal status – the bodhi tree and the meditation seat beneath it, or else the Buddha's footprints or sandals. (*Above left*: Presentation of Rahula to his father Shakyamuni, Amaravati, India, 2nd century)

After Shakyamuni's death, his ashes were interred in eight stupas by the eight groups of his followers assembled at Kushinagara (the number eight symbolizing the universe as the four cardinal directions and four mid-points). It was the Mauryan Emperor Ashoka who first made Buddhism a state religion in the 3rd century BC; his patronage encouraged new waves of artistic and architectural production. Legends accredit Ashoka with the building of some 84,000 stupas, but even if this is a great exaggeration, it should be remembered that even the tiniest fragment of ash, or remnant of anything that once belonged to the Buddha or to a great Buddhist teacher was considered a genuine relic. In any case, many of Ashoka's monuments were surely commemorative rather than relic stupas. Some were depicted with archaic signs of good luck, such as the snake, parasol and royal elephants. Ashoka also had pillars set up throughout the empire that were inscribed with Buddhist teachings and topped by beasts. The most famous of these show a strong Persian influence in the form of the solar lions, whose eyes were originally studded with gems, and the pillars themselves hark back to the memorial columns of ancient Mesopotamia. (*Above right*: Lion capital of Ashokan pillar, polished sandstone, Sarnath, India, 250 BC; *below*: Elephants worshipping a stupa, Amaravati, India, 2nd century)

More abstractly, the Wheel of the Law represented the *dharma*, usually accompanied by two deer to symbolize the first discourse in the Deer Park at Sarnath. (*Left*: The Wheel of the Law, from the roof of Jokhang Temple, Lhasa, Tibet)

Western influences culminated in the late Hellenistic style of Gandhara, an isolated pocket of artistic legacy left behind by Alexander on his abortive attempt to subdue the Indian subcontinent. Gandhara figures display a realism of dress and physical form eschewed by the sublime and truly Indian style of the Gupta period, the golden age of Buddhist art. (*Above*: Turning the Wheel of the Law, Gandhara, Pakistan, 2nd–3rd century; *right*: Turning the Wheel of the Law, Gupta, Sarnath, India, 6th century)

Life in the Sangha

In Buddhist countries it is generally considered a great honour and blessing to have a son become a novice as young as six or seven years of age, a fact that the West finds hard to understand. One reason for the Buddhist attitude is that a son in the Robe earns great merit for his family, and for his mother in particular. In Burma, it is customary for boys dressed as princes to re-enact Gautama's renunciation before becoming novices.

Nuns do exist in Buddhism, though are less numerous and generally more reclusive. (*Above left*: Ordination ceremony, Pagan, Burma; *above right*: Tibetan nuns at Ta-Tshang nunnery, Sikkim, in 1904)

From earliest times, Buddhism was patronized by the merchant classes, who occupied the lower levels of the Hindu caste system. The symbolic core of the mutually beneficial relationship of monastery and community is nourishment: both groups supply sustenance, the monks spiritual and the lay-people material. The *sangha* relied

on alms for its living, gathered either from the daily alms round or from visitors to the monastery. This is still the rule in the Theravada. At any ceremony the monks perform, such as blessing a marriage, funeral or new house, they will usually receive gifts, including food. (*Below left*: The Buddha receiving alms, detail from lacquer and gold leaf panel, the library of Suan Pakkard Palace, Bangkok, Thailand; *below right*: Monks receiving food, Wat Lampang Luang, Lampang, Thailand)

A boy who spends his early years in the monastery gains not only a good education, but also has the opportunity to make contacts which, should he later choose to leave the Robe, would stand him in good stead. It is still the custom in Theravada countries, particularly in Thailand, for young men to enter the monastery at least once in their lives for a limited period, often during the annual three-month rainy season retreat. So established is this custom that employers will grant time off for it.

Life in the *sangha* is traditionally very regimented. Monks should eat their one daily meal by noon, and offerings of food or drink given to images should likewise be made only in the morning.

In addition, a monk should observe 227 vows – including prohibitions on handling money and watching entertainment – which are recited in their entirety by the community each full moon. Traditionally only a limited number of possessions is allowed: a robe, an alms bowl, needle and cotton, and a water filter. Although such rules still apply in Theravada sects, nowadays they tend to be less strictly observed in Buddhism as a whole. Monastic life is devoted to meditation, study, debate and eventually teaching. (*Top right*: Monastic debate, Drepung Monastery, Tibet; *above*: Young monks at study, Wat Mahathat, Nakhon Si Thammarat, Thailand; *right*: Library interior, Szechuan Monastery, China)

The Stupa

A stupa is a solid reliquary mound derived from the ancient tumuli of India, which had been royal tombs since earliest times. Miniature stupas were used as reliquaries or votive offerings. The pagodas of the Far East are versions of the stupa, the name being a derivation from the Sri Lankan term *dagoba* ('relic store'). (*Above*: The Great Stupa, Sanchi, India, 3rd century BC, and detail from the gateway, 1st century BC; *left*: Bronze and turquoise votive stupa, India, 12th century; *far left*: Yakushi-ji Pagoda, Nishinokyo, Nara, Japan, 8th century)

The first cult object in Buddhism was the bodhi tree, or cuttings from it, which were taken wherever a major seat of the new faith was established. This custom will have dovetailed well with existing animistic tree-worshipping cults, and allowed the new faith to take root. The tree was then stylized and used as the crowning member or finial of the stupa.

Symbolically the dome of the stupa (the *anda*) refers to the Cosmic Egg from which the universe sprang, and the stupa thus belongs to that type of sacred building which represents the origin and centre of the world, whereas the finial (or *yasti*) is a version of the *axis mundi* which unites heaven and earth. The relics are commonly called *bija*, meaning 'seed', a term which implies the life-giving force, and transforms the funeral mound from a monument to the dead to an inspiration for the living.

There are four categories of stupa: those containing ashes or belongings of the Buddha; those containing ashes or belongings of an important teacher; those commemorating an event; and those donated as an act of merit by a lay-person. The stupa is found

everywhere Buddhism spread, and is the religion's major contribution to world architecture. The variety of form is enormous and each country has a different name for similar structures: all-seeing *chortens* in the Himalayas; monolithic pagodas in Burma; and gracefully attenuated *chedis* in Thailand. (*Bottom left*: The Great Stupa, Bodhnath, Nepal, 1st century BC; *above*: Shwedagon Pagoda, prototype of all later Burmese stupas, Pagan, Burma, 11th century; *above right*: chedi, Wat Suan Dork, Chiang Mai, Thailand)

All phenomena are interrelated; thus in the macrocosm the levels of the stupa symbolize the five elements (base = earth, dome = water, spire = fire, parasol capital = air, finial = ether or Buddha nature), and in the microcosm of the human nervous system, the five principal *chakras* and the five senses – smell, taste, sight, touch, and hearing respectively. A modern stupa, marking the establishment of a *dharma* centre in England, combines traditional elements of design. (*Right*: Peace Pagoda, Milton Keynes, England)

Places of Power

Initially inhabited as retreats during the three-month rainy season, caves and rock-cut sanctuaries were among the early communities' first permanent dwellings. They were often located near trade routes to facilitate donation and pilgrimage, or at places already sanctioned as holy by indigenous cults. Religious art always tends towards conservatism and cave sanctuaries continued to be excavated long after the ability to build freestanding structures had been developed. Some early freestanding temples show clear traces of both cave and stupa in their design; others developed as communal extensions of the isolated hermit's retreat. (*Above*: Salset Caves, print, 19th century; *above left*: Chandi Sewu Temple, Java, 8th century; *below left*: Spirit house, Thailand; *below and top right*: Tiger's Nest Monastery, Bhutan)

All the religious groups in ancient India used anchorite caves – over two thousand have been discovered – and the technical feats of quarrying thousands of tons of stone and decorating the interiors with murals and carvings was considerable, often involving large numbers of both monks and laymen. Buddhist cave sanctuaries were often carved with ornamental motifs, such as wooden roofbeams, which had no structural purpose but served the nostalgic function of recalling the halcyon days during the Buddha's lifetime when the community lived simply in forest glades. As well as providing a link with the past, their design represented an architecture of weighty mass that encourages

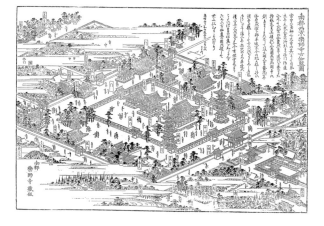

introversion and is thus eminently suited to the life of contemplation.

Temples would often be associated with relic stupas and were placed adjacent to the living quarters of the custodian monks, providing a place for images to be housed and pilgrims to assemble. In time, with the spread of the faith and the patronage of the wealthy and powerful, magnificent complexes of monasteries and temples arose all over the Buddhist world, some becoming veritable citadels of the sacred. (*Above left*: Yakushi Temple, Nara, Japan, 7th century; *above right*: Lung yen Monastery, China, in 1939; *right*: Thikse Gompa, Ladakh)

Worship

The original Theravada rationalism soon gave way to a teaching more suited to the needs of men and women living in the everyday world beyond the monastery walls. A more overtly religious approach, incorporating faith and devotional sentiment, shaped the worship of the lay population. As teachers and embodiments of the *dharma*, monks are a prime focus of a devotion expressed practically by both laymen and royalty. Gifts can range from food and 'money trees', which link the symbol of the bodhi tree with the practical necessities of life, to the sponsoring of religious festivals and building projects. Such gifts not only ensure the continuity of the *dharma* in the world, but also bring the donor merit and good fortune in both this and future lives. (*Above left*: Lay offerings to a monk, Burma; *above right*: illustration from the Book of Royal Donations, Burma, 19th century; *below*: Monk receiving 'money tree', Burma)

In communities still largely bound by traditional areas of occupation and limited mobility, pilgrimage still serves a valuable social function, in addition to its benefits for the individual's *karma*. It unites the community by providing the opportunity for travel, celebration, seeing relatives and friends and settling important affairs. (*Above*: Pilgrims visiting the Potala, Lhasa, Tibet)

Monks in their turn give teachings and blessings to the faithful, infusing purity and spiritual power into the world of everyday life even by their very presence, a transference of energy known as *darshan* ('seeing'). Within the wide spectrum of devotional practices in Buddhism, many archaic elements remain, such as the worship of a different shrine for each day of the week at Burma's most important pagoda, the Shwedagon in Rangoon. (*Above*: The Dalai Lama giving public blessing, New Year, Dharamsala; *above left*: Shrine worship, Shwedagon Pagoda, Rangoon, Burma)

At its heart, though, Buddhism remains essentially an individual affair, involving disciplines similar to those found in the other great religions: a simple and straightforward morality based on loving-kindness towards all forms of life, various means of mental discipline such as meditation, and an attitude of devotion cultured by reverence for the image of the founder of the faith. (*Below left*: Ladakhi woman with rosary; *below*: Instructing children in worship, Wat Suan Dork, Chiang Mai, Thailand)

Festival and Ritual

Most Buddhist festivals are lunar; symbolically, the moon is closely associated with water, and both are feminine images of the unconscious and the infinite, nature's hidden power of regeneration. Water is one of the offerings placed before deities each day in many Buddhist temples and homes. (*Right*: Bronze infant Buddha, Todaiji, Japan, lustrated with holy water purified with special herbs, in honour of his birth)

Monks officiate at more private functions and important rites of passage such as marriage and the blessing of foundations, where the chanting of the scriptures is an important part of the purification and blessing. For a parent, ordination of the son as a novice is perhaps the most treasured life ritual, and the supreme act of generosity. (*Above*: Mass ordination of novices in Burma, 1898; *right*: A Ladakhi bride at her wedding ceremony)

In the Kathmandu Valley of Nepal, an area of extraordinary religious syncretism where Hindus, Buddhists and sacrificial cults share temples and images known under different names, the image of Matsyendranath, a local version of the *bodhisattva* Avalokiteshvara, is still processed in a spectacular chariot festival today. Buddhist images are sometimes believed to possess distinct personalities and miraculous powers, and in areas where traditional local beliefs still predominate, they are occasionally moved from temple to temple, or processed like the saints of Catholicism. (*Top right*: Matsyendranath Festival, Patan, Nepal, 19th century)

The single most important Buddhist festival is Visakha Puja, the April full moon, which simultaneously celebrates Shakyamuni's birth, Enlightenment and death. In Thailand, an April festival associated with Visakha Puja is Songkran, the astrological New Year. What was originally a sedate three-day celebration. in which merit was made by visiting the temple and bathing the hands of elders and parents with holy water, has become in modern times a raucous water-carnival, in which the usually stringent rules of Thai social formality are temporarily relaxed. April is the hottest month of the year in Thailand, and another purpose of Songkran is to encourage the celestial dragons, bringers of rain, to bless the earth when they witness the human squandering of precious water resources in their honour. Other Buddhist ceremonies express a whole culture's aesthetic, such as the Japanese tea ceremony, a fastidious celebration of the timeless perfection of the present moment. (*Left*: Songkran Carnival, Chiang Mai, Thailand; *below left*: 'Guests praising the decorations and utensils in the tea room', Toshikata, Japan, late 19th century; *below right*: Foundation ceremony for a private house in Kandy, Sri Lanka)

The Vajrayana

No other single school has developed such spectacular and arcane rituals as the esoteric Mahayana school known as the Vajrayana ('The Way of the Adamantine Thunderbolt') practised in Tibet, and thence the other Himalayan countries. Buddhism was introduced into Tibet by the great Indian yogi Padmasambhava in the eighth century, and Vajrayana is a complex mixture of Indian transcendental philosophy and esoteric ritual derived both from Tantric sources of north-east India and Tibet's indigenous shamanistic religion

of Bon-Po. Linked to an ancient Central Asian tradition, Bon-Po provided much of the vocabulary that expressed the Mahayana vision, including masked spirit dances, rituals using human bones and skull-caps, communal exorcism, liturgical music, and offerings sculpted out of yak butter, one of the country's most treasured commodities. (*Above left*: Masked dance, Hemis Gompa, Ladakh; *above right*: Exorcism ritual, Namgyal Monastery, Dharamsala; *left*: Making a butter sculpture, Namgyal Monastery; *below*: Puja ceremony, Nyingma Monastery, Darjeeling, India)

Under Buddhist influence, the raw cosmic powers were allied to the *bodhisattvas* and a pantheon of peaceful and wrathful deities, and were invoked for the benefit and protection of all beings. Ceremonies of universal purification, especially at New Year, are an important ritual. Much Tibetan life was governed by the daily eight-hour trances and pronouncements of the State Oracle, spokesman for the awesomely powerful spirit-protector Pehar Gyalpo and his principal emissary to Tibet, Dorje Drakden. The institution is still active in Dharamsala, north India, the headquarters of the Dalai Lama and the Tibetan peoples in exile. (*Right*: Fire *puja*, Tashilumpo Gompa, Shigatse, Tibet; *below*: Preparation of the State Oracle, Tibet)

The liturgical music of the Vajrayana centres on resonant bass chanting, and is used to summon, appease or banish elemental energies, or to induce the spirit to leave the body and travel in the astral realms. The complex deities with many limbs and heads, often studded with coral and turquoise, are cast in bronze, a skill the Vajrayana developed to great effect, while deities and mandalas painted on cotton and mounted on silk (*thankas*) constitute some of the finest Buddhist art. It is sometimes said that Tibetan and thence Vajrayana art is, for all its strangeness, essentially provincial Chinese work, but in fact nothing could be further from the truth. As with all aspects of its extraordinary world-view, Vajrayana developed a profoundly

idiosyncratic artistic style whose transcendental inspiration owed little to the imperialistic influence of its more powerful neighbour. (*Below left*: Ceremonial chanting summoning deities; *below right*: *Bodhisattva*, Thikse Gompa, Ladakh)

Macrocosm, Microcosm and Mandala

The prime aim of Mahayana iconography was to enshrine its doctrine of the interrelatedness of all phenomena, and to allude to the underlying and interpenetrating Reality in which all phenomena inhere. The most succinct formulation of the *dharma* is the Wheel of Life, in which the twelve stages of the chain of conditioning encircle the six realms of existence. These in turn revolve around the three forces of *samsara*: ignorance, desire and hatred – symbolized by the pig, cock and snake – the basic emotional impulses which keep us attached to the phenomenal and unsatisfactory universe. The whole illusory show is held in the abysmal grip of the master of illusion, Mahakala, the Lord of Time. (*Right*: Wheel of Life, gouache on cloth, Tibet, 18th century)

The cosmic hierarchy was expressed through geometric mandalas as levels of consciousness descending into matter through a graded series of increasing densities. These mandalas were used in meditation and visualization exercises to facilitate the return journey from gross matter to the unboundedness of the Void. Three-dimensional models of the cosmic hierarchy are made – usually representations of Mount Meru, the centre and apex of the Buddhist universe – either as temple offerings or occasionally as entire temple sites, such as Borobodur, the largest Buddhist shrine in the world. In Tibetan culture, mandalas are made of coloured sand representing the universe to be purified each new year. In a fitting analogue of the cosmic process, weeks of creative effort are swept away after a ritual lasting but a few short hours. (*Above left*: Monks making a sand mandala, Namgyal Monastery, Dharamsala; *above right*: Ground-plan of Borobodur, largest stupa in the world, Java, 8th century)

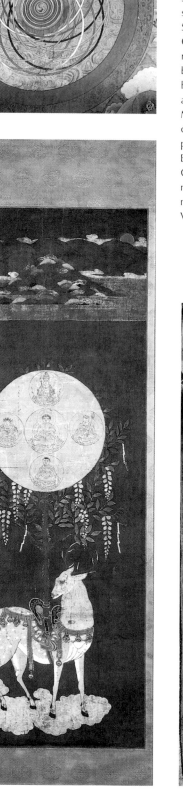

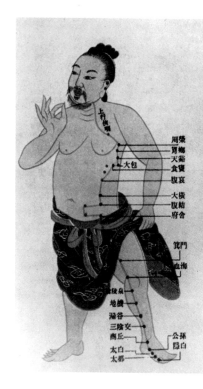

The continuum of the cosmic hierarchy could be expressed abstractly, or more concretely as orders of deities radiating out from the Absolute, which is personified as the supreme Buddha. Sometimes the symbols of existing religions such as Shintoism were adopted or adapted. On the understanding of the microcosmic mandala of the human body are based both the martial and healing arts of Buddhism, such as acupuncture and massage. (*Above left*: Mandala depicting the origin of the cosmos through the evolution of the planets and elements, Paro Dzong, Bhutan; *right*: Acupuncture chart, China, 18th century; *left*: Kasuga Deer mandala, Japan, 15th century; *below*: mandala of the supreme Buddha Vajrasattva, Tibet, 18th century)

Protectors

The jungle countries of southern and eastern Asia have always been rich mines of animistic lore, and many local protective spirits were adopted by Buddhism as it spread. In conformity with the *dharma*'s tolerance – a result of its non-dual perspective on life – the Buddhist world view has always sought to include pre-existing beliefs and practices rather than to banish or alienate them. Thus spirits associated with trees and fertility were incorporated into myths of Gautama's birth; serpents and dragons, always a beneficent supernatural presence in the East, protect Buddhist teachings and temples, and celestial musicians and dancers grace the walls of complexes such as Angkor Wat. In this way, Buddhism flourished as a natural outgrowth, albeit more refined and significant, of the existing cultural mulch, and as a result could be easily assimilated by cultures converted to the *dharma*. The sacred inner sanctum must always be protected from the profane outer world of impurity and death – the threshold and entrance are always the most vulnerable points. Protectors may appear as deities awaiting sacrifice or warriors thirsting for battle. (*Top left*: Yakshi, fertility spirit, Sanchi, India, 1st century BC; *top right*: dancers, Angkor Wat, Cambodia, 9th century; *above left*: Cave guardians, Lung Men, China, 5th century; *left*: Ordination hall, northern Thailand)

In these and many other cases, the lines between what is Hindu and what is Buddhist iconography are often blurred, myths and images being shared as part of the vast pan-Indian reservoir of imaginative life. Indeed, temple sites may be sequentially, or even simultaneously, worshipped by both Hindu and Buddhist, with no sense of friction. Garuda, a mythical man-bird, attendant of the Hindu deity Vishnu, appears on many temple lintels as a protector in the Himalayas.

Many protectors are represented as peaceful beings, suffused with a soft and happy beauty to show the sensuous bliss that awaits those who penetrate to the heart of life. Many are female, expressing the mysterious and irrepressibly fecund power of nature. Male protectors, in conformity with ancient Indian ideals of beauty and wholeness, exhibit an androgenous grace, and it is often impossible to tell from the face alone the gender of the being.

This type of representation perfectly suited the artist's intentions to portray an energy that is beyond the normal divisions of our dualistic vision and managed to combine the sensual and the spiritual in works that are, at their best, breathtakingly lovely. (*Above left*: Garuda, woodcarving, Nepal, 18th century; *above right*: Apsaras, female protecting spirit, Angkor Wat, 9th century; *left*: Avalokiteshvara, bronze, Nepal; *right*: Kichijoten, wood, Japan, 12th century)

Name and Form

In Buddhism, the entire universe of relative existence is known as the realm of *namarupa* – 'name and form' – and it is through the correct understanding of sound and substance that its secrets are unlocked. The supreme man-made form is the Buddha image. Beautiful though they usually are, to the believer considerations of aesthetics are secondary, and the charm of an image (*rupa*) does not derive only from the sensory level. The image is somehow mysteriously charged with the power of the *dharma*, and in this capacity provides both a focus for the cultivation of refined emotions – such as loving-kindness, reverence and devotion – and also a springboard from which the mind can ascend in contemplation. Buddha *rupas* are traditionally made by hereditary families of artists and craftsmen, who are considered to be time-tested channels through which the sacred forms can be made manifest. In the creation of a *rupa*, the craftsman should mindfully follow a routine of purification and invocation before visualizing the divine form to be represented. Form is structured by sound; the most perfect man-made sound is the chanted scripture, through which the mind and senses are purified and the world of name and form can be understood in its fullness. Thus the arts of the manuscript – calligraphy, block-printing and illumination – have always been of great importance in Buddhism. Monastic libraries are traditionally the repository of all aspects of knowledge – religious,

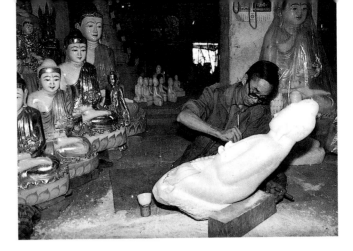

medical, administrative – as were their counterparts in medieval Christendom. (*Top*: Making a Buddha image, Rangoon, Burma; *above right*: Block printing the scriptures, Tibet; *right*: Printing block library, destined not to survive the Cultural Revolution, Szechuan, China; *below*: 'Perfection of Wisdom sutras', Nepal, 12th century)

In the fine arts, Buddhist calligraphic skills linked the philosophy of the *dharma* to the refined sensibility of the Chinese landscape tradition. Ch'an, the Chinese meditative school that became Zen in Japan, was founded by Bodhidharma, a monk from India, always protrayed as a somewhat lugubrious character with bushy eyebrows. Some of the Far-Eastern representations of nature (often featuring bamboo, the epitome of strength through flexibility) are justly celebrated. The best capture the unity of form and emptiness expressed in the Zen aphorism that 'the trees show the bodily form of the wind', and manage directly to suggest the creativity of the Void, the inexhaustible freshness of the Buddha-field. (*Right*: Bamboo in the wind, Wu Chen, China; *below*: Bodhidharma, Japan; *below right*: Boat at anchor by reeds, China, 15th century)

Sound and Silence

Life at both gross and subtle levels is movement: movement involves sound. And just as all form is sculpted in stillness, so all sound is grounded in silence. Tibetan prayer-wheels containing texts printed on rice paper or cotton send silent supplication to the gods who themselves are manifest as vibrational energies in the realms of subtle sound, and who can be invoked

by the correct intonation of their harmonic bodies as chants and *mantras*. Shakyamuni observed that between any two moments in time, an infinite number of 'mind-moments' occur, and these in turn arise out of the immaculate void that is our real nature. This subjective awareness of the undisturbed ground of activity is fundamental to the oriental disposition, and has influenced all aspects of its culture. Eastern classical music incorporates quarter tones and deliberate tonal spacing to allow for minute subdivision and thence silence, and its concept of harmony comprises not only the component parts of the music itself, but also the fact that tonal rhythms should be in concord with the other planetary rhythms of time and space. Thus in ancient India particular types of music were deemed to be

suited to particular times of day, seasons and places, and all music had a liturgical purpose. In this way the healing power of sound, known to all cultures, was incorporated consciously and therapeutically into the structure of what we call music. Buddhist ritual instruments such as the conch and the drum should be played in such a way as to enliven rhythms in the physiology of the listener and to make full use of the stillness between each note. Similar considerations lie behind the phrasing of the Gregorian Chant of the West. (*Above*: Prayer-wheels at Palabu Temple, with the Potala in the background, Lhasa, Tibet; Conch-shell trumpet, 19th century; *below*: One of the 37 *nats*, spirits who dwell in the subtle realms of sound, personified as a musician, Burma, 19th century; Service at Manpukuge Monastery, Japan)

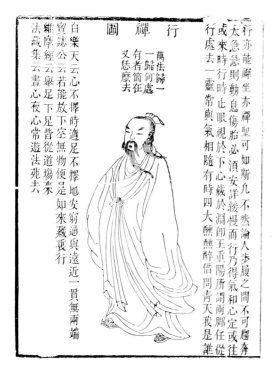

行禪圖

萬法歸一
一歸何處
又恁麼去

有者箇在

白樂天云心不擇時適足不擇地安窮通與遠近一貫無兩端
寶誌公云若能放下空無物便是如來藏裏行
維摩經云舉足下足皆從道場來
法藏集云晝心夜心常遊法苑去

行亦能禪坐亦禪聖可如斯几不然論人步履之間不可趨奔
太急急則動息傷怡必須安詳緩慢而行乃得氣和心定或往
或來時行時止眼視於下心藏於淵即王重陽所謂兩脚任從
行處去一靈常與氣相隨有時四大醺醺醉借問青天我是誰

Mental silence, the culmination of all internalized sound, is the outcome of meditation, a procedure by which images, thoughts and sounds are traced to their root in the matrix of inner quietude. The silent mind is achieved through long retreats when the world of the senses is left far behind. Nor is the lucid equanimity that results from retreat limited to the conducive surroundings of forest or cave. As Gautama's own cycle of retreat, solitariness and eventual compassionate return indicates, for the wise the tranquil state persists under all conditions of life. (*Top right*: Anchorite walled up in the 'Caves of Happiness', Tibet; *above*: Walking meditation, China; *right*: Zen monk, Japan)

Changing the Body

Death is the only sure thing in life, and growth proceeds through change, which is the death of the old. Even the continuity of the daily flow of time is illusory, in reality there is a momentariness that proceeds through the birth and death of each moment. Buddhists have always practised cremation, and unlike the Semitic religions, there is no attempt to preserve the body in expectation of a future resurrection at the Day of Judgment. The basic fact of physical impermanence cannot be denied and judgment, in the sense of suffering the effects of our actions, is experienced moment to moment, life to life. Yet this is not mere materialism. To the Buddhist, physical death is like a door marked 'exit' from one side and 'entrance' from the other, and belief in reincarnation is central to the early Buddhism which, in conformity with the imaginative boldness of the Indian psyche, was quite at home in expanded vistas transcending all common-sense notions of time, space and causality. (*Top left*: Amida, Buddha of the Western paradise, attended by *bodhisattvas*, Japan, 13th century; *left*: Enma-o, King of the Underworld, judges the dead, Japan, 11th–12th century; *below*: Burning of paper objects as part of a Shui Lu soul mass, China).

When the *dharma* travelled to China and thence Japan, it encountered a very different mind-set. The Chinese, renowned for their down-to-earth pragmatism and dislike of abstraction, were already steeped in ancestor worship, a world-view that seeks to maintain a quasi-material continuity between the realms of life and the afterlife. They were naturally at home with their hierarchy of bureaucratic gods who, like a celestial civil service, are believed to control and judge the affairs of men. It was therefore inevitable that some Mahayana schools in China and Japan grafted indigenous ideas of prolonged afterlife in heaven or hell on to the imported religion.

In Thailand, where young men can enter the monastery for short periods, it is not unusual for a bereaved son or nephew to spend time as a monk to ease his relative's passage beyond death. In terms of *karma*, this earns him and his dead relative merit; in terms of psychology, it also allows him a public time of grieving in a disinterested and supportive environment. Tibetan high lamas traditionally leave some sort of a prophecy as to where they will reincarnate; the young boy suspected of being the new *tulku* undergoes various tests, including the identification of personal belongings from his previous life, before he is accepted as genuine. Tibetan *tulkus* are now being born in the West, a sign that despite the attempted destruction of the Tibetan life and spirit by the Chinese, the *dharma* itself is immortal.

(*Top left*: Memorial *chorten* containing the heart of the 16th Gyalwa Karmapa, Rumtek Monastery, Gangtok, Sikkim; *top right*: Mourner entering the *sangha*, with the coffin behind, Thailand; *above*: Street opera in Singapore, performed for the deceased; *right*: Osel Torres, the first Tibetan *tulku* to be reincarnated in the West)

Buddhism in the Western Arts

The influence of Eastern art on the West began in earnest at the time of great colonial expansion at the end of the eighteenth and nineteenth centuries. In this process the art of India, the home of Buddhism, has always been something of a poor relation. India's art is inseparable from its religions, and these were long viewed by the Christian West as heathen doctrines clothed in multi-armed, hybrid forms that were monstrous and even diabolic. Latterly, with the lowering of the barriers of

Victorian cultural and religious prejudice, the austere taste of modernism has looked with disfavour on the baroque and ornate emotionalism that informs so much Indian-derived art, a disfavour still visible in the salesroom today. The arts of China and Japan, on the other hand,

greatly influenced by Buddhist ideas, and by the late nineteenth century the interest in Orientalism had introduced Buddhism to Western artistic circles. The luxury of Gautama's early life appealed to the contemporary taste for decadence, his renunciation to Victorian family sentiment, while the mysticism of his maturity attracted artists like Odilon Redon. A less direct influence can be seen in works of painters such as Whistler, whose experiments in tonal effect produced paintings with a strong atmosphere of what Buddhists call 'emptiness'. In literature, Edwin Arnold's poem about the Buddha, 'The Light of Asia' (1879) was a seminal influence; the illustrations from an edition of 1926 give Shakyamuni a distinctly Christlike appearance. More recently, *Siddhartha* (1930) one of the most popular works of the visionary novelist Herman Hesse, has influenced generations of spiritual seekers. *Siddhartha* was turned into a highly successful cult film in 1970.

('The Tortoise and the Birds', Caxton's Aesop; 'Gautama in the Palace', Hesse's own illustration from an Indian edition of *Siddhartha*; *Buddha's Renunciation*, Nicholas Chevalier, 1884; *A woman, dove-eyed, young*, Hamzeh Carr, 1926; Still from 'Siddhartha', Conrad Rookes, 1970; *Buddha*, Odilon Redon, *c.* 1905; *Nocturne in Blue and Silver: Cremorne Lights*, Whistler, 1872)

have always been more accessible to the West. The culture that informed them posed no threat, and their style was acceptable in European interiors. Close trading links with Europe allowed oriental taste to accompany tea and silk westwards from the end of the seventeenth century on. This influence was strong in America as well, where commercial contact was compounded by geographical proximity.

Buddhism had exerted a limited influence from early times. Many famous collections of fables echo the Jataka Tales, stories of Shakyamuni's previous lives. German idealist thinkers at the beginning of the nineteenth century, such as Hegel and Kant, were

Glossary

bodhisattva: 'Pure-minded one', who has dedicated his life to the welfare and Enlightenment of all sentient beings

Bodhi tree, bo tree: The tree – a type of fig – under which Gautama attained Enlightenment, in the garden at Bodh Gaya

chedi: A Thai stupa

chorten: A Tibetan stupa

dharma: The natural law; the Truth; the teaching of the Enlightened Ones

dhyani buddha: A celestial buddha of the Mahayana pantheon

mahaparinirvana: The death of an enlightened being

Mahayana: The Buddhist schools followed in the Himalayas, China, Japan, Korea and Indonesia

nirvana: Enlightenment while living

rupa: A buddha image

samsara: The phenomenal world of impermanent form

samskara: The psychological and emotional residue of past experience giving rise to our latent tendencies

sangha: The community of monks and nuns

sati: Mindfulness

shunyata: Emptiness; the Void; the Unbounded; the ultimate Reality of life

sila: Morality

sutra: An aphoristic scripture, containing the words of the Buddha

Theravada: The oldest Buddhist school, followed in Burma, Sri Lanka & Thailand

tulku: A reincarnated Tibetan lama

upaya: Skilful means in teaching

Further Reading

Ajahn Chah, Bodhinyana, Bung Wai Forest Monastery, 1982

Ajahn Sumedho, Mindfulness: the Path to Deathlessness, Amaravati, 1987

Bechert, H. & R. Gombrich, The World of Buddhism, Thames and Hudson, 1984

Conze, E., Buddhism, Cassirer, 1957

——, Buddhist Thought in India, Allen & Unwin, 1962

——, Buddhist Texts Through the Ages, Shambhala, 1990

Da Free John, Nirvanasara, Dawn Horse Press, 1982

Disciples of Ajahn Chah, Seeing the Way, Amaravati Publications, 1989

Evans Wenz, W.Y., The Tibetan Book of the Dead, OUP, 1957

——, The Tibetan Book of the Great Liberation, OUP, 1954

——, Tibetan Yoga and Secret Doctrines, OUP, 1935

Francis, H.T. & E.J. Thomas, Jataka Tales, Jaico Publishing, 1970

Fremantle, F. & Chogyam Trungpa, The Tibetan Book of the Dead, Shambhala, 1975

Humphries, C., Buddhism, Pelican, 1971

Mascaro, J. (trans), The Dhammapada, Penguin, 1978

Price, A.F. & Wong Mou Lam (trans), The Diamond Sutra & the Sutra of Hui Neng, Shambhala, 1969

Rahula, W., What The Buddha Really Taught, Gordon Fraser, 1959

Reps, P., Zen Flesh, Zen Bones, Pelican, 1957

Powell, A. & G. Harrison, Living Buddhism, BMP, 1989

Snellgrove, D., The Image of the Buddha, Unesco Press, 1978

Suzuki, D.T. (trans), The Lankavatara Sutra, Routledge, 1973

——, Essays in Zen Buddhism, Rider, 1973

——, Outlines of Mahayana Buddhism, Schocken Books Inc, 1963

Trungpa, Chogyam, Cutting through Spiritual Materialism, Shambhala, 1977

——, The Myth of Freedom, Shambhala, 1976

Tulka, Tarthang, Gesture of Balance, Dharma, 1977

Thich Nhat Hanh, Being Peace, Parallax Press, 1989

Acknowledgments

The following abbreviations are used: a above, b below, c centre, l left, r right:

Stuart Ackland 75b; Archaeological Museum, Amaravati 70al; Koninklijk Instituut voor de Tropen, Amsterdam 76al; Bendigo Art Gallery (photo Emily Lane) 94ar; Brian Beresford 62a, 80b, 82al, 83c, 93c; Birmingham Museum and Art Gallery 17; Prince of Wales Museum of Western Art, Bombay 8, 54bl; Museum of Fine Arts, Boston 89a,br; Indian Museum, Calcutta 66al; Camera Press, London 91b; J. Charbonnier/Agence Top 58b; Pra Sing, Luang Monastery, Chiengmai/photo Breezewood Foundation 67b; China News Agency 77cr, 86c; Colnaghi, London 85bl; Archaeological Department, Colombo 63; Royal Library Copenhagen/Photo J. Prip-Møller 73b, 88 second from bottom, right, 92br;

Werner Forman Archive 46, 47, (Philip Goldman Collection) 25; Richard Gombrich 81br; Graham Harrison 36r–37, 40–41, 45, 53r, 54al, 56a, 60; Hans Hinz 69b; David Hughes 90br; Martin Hürlimann 59, 74ar; Kabul Museum (photo Josephine Powell) 65; Kyoto: Chionin 92a; Joruriji 87br; Koryuju 35a; Shohoji temple 26; Central Museum, Lahore 67ar; Richard Lannoy 50b ; London: British Film Institute 94br; British Library 56–7, 66b, 78ar, 88b; British Museum 4, 9, 12, 62b, 70b, 71l, 84a, 87al, 89bl; Horniman Museum 92bl; India Office Library (Photo J. Claude White) 72ar, (Photo J. G. Scott) 80c, (Bell Archive) 91ar; Jamyang Meditation Centre 93b; Tate Gallery 95b; Office of Tibet 83bl; Tibet Foundation 79ar, 82ar,cl,br, 84cl, 88 second from top; Victoria and Albert Museum 34, 68br, 81bl, 85br, 87bl; Los Angeles County Museum of Art 31; Zaw Lwin 33, 42, 72al; Staatliche Museum für

Völkerkunde, Munich 15; Nara: Chuguji Convent 35b; Horyuji 19; Yakushiji 75cl; John Okell 78al; Ashmolean Museum, Oxford 90bl; Paris: Bibliothèque Nationale 91l; Musée Guimet 68al, 81a Musée d'Orsay 95a; Peshawar Museum, Pakistan (photo Josephine Powell, 68bl; Josephine Powell 39, 74al; Private Collection 10, 74cr; 90ar; M. Sakamoto 80a; Archaeological Museum, Sarnath (Photo Martin Hürlimann) 70ar, (photo Josephine Powell) 71b; Alistair Shearer 36a,b, 38, 41r, 48, 49, 52–3, 54–55, 56b, 61a,b, 64, 66ar,cr, 67c, 68ar, 69ar, 71a, 72bl,br, 73a,c, 74br, 75al,ar, 76ar,bl,br, 77a,b, 78c,b, 79al,cl,br, 81cl, 83ar,br, 85al, 86al,ar,ab, 87ar, 88a, 90al, 93al,ar, and cover; Luca Invernizzi Tettoni/ Photobank 44; Tokyo National Museum 7; Henry Wilson 43; Yakushi Temple, Japan 50a (photo Toshio Watanabe) 51; Zurich: Museum Rietburg 29; Museum für Völkerkunde 23.